I SAW CONGO

by

E. R. MOON

THE UNITED CHRISTIAN MISSIONARY SOCIETY
INDIANAPOLIS

PRINTED IN THE UNITED STATES OF AMERICA
1952

To

My wife, the full partner in all my missionary labors on the foreign field and in America.

CONTENTS

FOREWORD - - - - - - - - - - - - - - 7

A TWELVE THOUSAND MILE HONEYMOON TRIP - 9

PART ONE—RIVER AND JUNGLE TRAIL - - - - 21

Chapter I—*Steamboat on the Congo* - - - 23

Chapter II—*The Game Trail* - - - - - 31

Chapter III—*Snakes, Fish, Insects* - - - 45

PART TWO—CONGO VILLAGE LIFE - - - - - 57

Chapter I—*The Congo Village* - - - - - 59

Chapter II—*Marriage Customs and Names* - 75

Chapter III—*Language and Communication* 87

Chapter IV—*Folk-Songs, Proverbs, Fables* - 97

PART THREE—CONGO'S OLD AND NEW FAITHS - 113

Chapter I—*Old Beliefs and Practices* - - - 115

Chapter II—*A New Faith Takes Root* - - 129

Chapter III—*A Mission Station Is Opened* - 147

SUNSET OR DAWN? - - - - - - - - - - 165

FOREWORD

My wife and I were missionaries in Congo from 1908 to 1923. Then, after I had taught missions for ten years and served as a pastor for five, we were asked to go to Jamaica. There we labored until I reached retirement age in 1944. Since then we have spent most of our time holding meetings among our churches. During the first week of each meeting I speak every night on some phase of Congo life and beliefs. These lectures have been well received and all our spare time is usually spoken for a full year in advance. Because of the continued demand for these lectures and the constant urging of friends, I have put in writing the materials used in these Congo talks.

Some of the customs and practices of which I write still persist, but many have passed away. Rapid changes are taking place in Congo life today. But the more one knows of the life and thinking of the Congolese in those earlier years, the better one can understand them today, and the more helpful one can be to them in this period of change. If these few chapters help toward a better understanding and appreciation of the Congo people, I shall be happy and feel amply repaid for the time spent in their preparation.

I want to thank Dr. Ross J. Griffeth, president of Northwest Christian College, whose encouragement has kept me at the job; Dr. Orval D. Peterson, pastor of the First Christian Church, Yakima, Washington, who has read the manuscript and made many valuable suggestions; and a host of friends who have helped in many ways toward the completion of the book.

Yours for a Christian Congo,

E. R. Moon

The correct pronunciation of Lonkundo, the language of the Central Congo area of this book, can be approximated by bearing in mind that the vowels are pronounced as in Latin, the consonants as in English, except that g is always hard and that c is pronounced as ch. When a word or syllable begins with m or n followed by a consonant, the sound is nasal, m being pronounced with the lips closed and n with the tongue against the roof of the mouth. The vowel sound of o is like a in awl. Stress is quite even on all syllables.

A TWELVE THOUSAND MILE
HONEYMOON TRIP

A ND A HALF FOUR-R-R . . . By the mark four-r-r . . .
Quarter less four," came ringing in through the
porthole, at measured intervals, in a rich Scotch brogue.
I thrust my head out and there on a little platform at-
tached to the side of the ship, silhouetted against the
sky in the dim light of the early morning, stood a tall,
well-built figure heaving the lead.

The ocean was calm. A lazy phosphorescent wave
sheared off from the prow of the ship like liquid silver
sprinkled with floating diamonds. It was evident that
land was near, for the soundings gradually grew less
and the ship proceeded very slowly. My wife and I
hurriedly dressed and went up on deck, thrilled with
the prospect of our first glimpse of Africa.

Dawn in the tropics does not tarry long. When we
reached the deck it was broad daylight. The smooth
sea was now light green in color. Nearby the dorsal fin
of a shark plowed through the surface of the water like
the conning tower of a miniature submarine. A flying
fish, inspired by fear to do the impossible, arose out of
the water, sailed away some distance with apparently
no idea of where it was going, and fell again into the
sea.

"And a deep thr-r-ee . . . Eighteen feet." The soundings indicated that the ship was as close into shore as it
dared go. The telegraph sounded and the engines ceased
the throbbing that had been continuous for nearly three

9

weeks. As the boat lost its way, the captain on the bridge blew a shrill whistle and with the rattling and clanking of the huge chain the anchor sank to the sandy floor of the sea. In some places for want of harbors it is necessary for ships to anchor out as we did that morning.

In the distance could be seen the surf breaking gently along Africa's "golden sands," for we were off the Gold Coast in the Gulf of Guinea. Just back of the sandy shoreline was the green forest, unbroken as far as the eye could see, except for one spot directly in front of us where stood a couple of houses with corrugated iron roofs. That was the post of some lone trader who had come seeking his fortune in this section of Africa which had been called the "white man's grave." In the early days no communication with the outside world was possible here except through an occasional visit of some steamer bringing in a new supply of trade goods and taking away a few barrels of palm oil and bags of kernels.

With emotions too deep for words at this our first sight of Africa, we stood in silence watching the listless swells roll lazily onto the beach where the white-capped surf elfs chased each other along the sandy shore. Finally I looked at Bessie and said, "Is it real? Is that Africa, or am I dreaming again my boyhood dream of sometime visiting the Dark Continent?"

Just a few months before that—'twas on Flag Day, June 14, 1908—Bessie Huntington, granddaughter of a pioneer Christian minister, and I had stood up in Castle Rock, Washington, before a young minister, my own brother Rupert, as he read the marriage ceremony. After the wedding, for a short honeymoon trip we chose to attend the Oregon Convention of Disciples of Christ and camped that week on the beautiful grounds at Turner.

The missionary speakers for the convention were Dr. and Mrs. Royal J. Dye, home on furlough after their second term of service in the Belgian Congo under the Foreign Christian Missionary Society. They thrilled the large crowds day after day with their stories of the Congo people and their deep spiritual needs. In one address Dr. Dye said, "Our mission in the Congo is in need of an evangelistic man who also knows something about building."

At the close of that session I said to Mrs. Moon, "What do you think about what the doctor said?" She answered, "It looks like a direct call to us." We had a talk with Dr. and Mrs. Dye. I said: "Doctor, I was raised in my father's carpenter shop and have worked at the trade. I am a graduate of Eugene Bible University and have spent two years in evangelistic work. Mrs. Moon, I believe, is well prepared in education and experience for missionary service. She is ready and willing to go. Do you think the Society would accept us?" He said, "You surely must be the answer to our prayers."

After further conference with us, Dr. Dye wired the Foreign Christian Missionary Society that he had found the couple they needed in the Congo. The answer came back, "No funds. Can't send them out this year." But no telegram like that ever stopped or even discouraged Dr. Dye. He went from the Oregon convention to California and in August we received word that he had secured two "living links" for our support, the Covina church and Mr. George Waters of the Pomona church.

We were asked to get ready to start for the Congo in time to visit our living links and attend the International Convention of Disciples of Christ to be held that year in New Orleans. After the convention we visited the headquarters of the Foreign Christian Missionary Society in Cincinnati. We were interviewed by newspaper reporters and the next day our pictures appeared on the front pages of two papers under big headlines: "Off on a Fourteen Thousand Mile Honeymoon Trip," and "To Spend Honeymoon Among Cannibals of Africa."

We spent a few days with the Dyes in their home in Ionia, Michigan, where they helped us with valuable information about our future work in Congo and aided us in our final preparation for the journey. Then we were off to New York and sailed on the White Star liner, *The Arabic,* in November, 1908. We spent a few days in Liverpool, England, completing our necessary outfit for life in the tropics, then sailed on the S.S. *Nigeria* for the Congo. And there on that day of our first glimpse of Africa we were anchored off the coast, wondering what awaited us in the dark recesses of its vast forests.

After a few hours we weighed anchor and were on our way again. Slowly and with many soundings our ship made its way in and out of several shallow Guinea Coast ports. By far the most interesting to us of all our ports of call was Calabar, situated on the right bank of the Calabar River near where it flows into the estuary which bears the same name. Along the bank of the river were located the customs office and the business houses; back on the hills were the government buildings, the hospital, and the Presbyterian Mission. Nestled in between the hills was the native quarter known as Duke Town. Calabar was a typical port-town village. Small houses were roofed with every conceivable kind of material from native thatching to the sides of empty oil cans. Along the narrow streets were many shops kept by natives, where were sold foods, European tools, utensils, and cloth. Most in evidence was the display of gay colored prints. One could easily imagine himself in the capital city of Crazy-land on Flag Day.

The kind and thoughtful captain put his gig at our disposal and Mrs. Moon and I went ashore to step for the first time on African soil. We could hardly have chosen a spot in Africa that would have meant more to new missionaries than Calabar. Here, on the one hand, were evidences of the best of Western civilization: orderly government, educational facilities, and one of the most historic Christian missions in all Africa—and a large native town enjoying these blessings. On the other hand, in the harbor still lay the hull of an old ship that had been used as a slave depot, a relic of greed and avarice that had cost Africa not less than one hundred million lives.

Leaving Calabar, our ship made a few more calls at less interesting ports, then sailed on to the southward. After several days, when about five degrees south of the Equator, the ocean suddenly lost its deep blue and changed to the color of weak coffee. We were sailing in the waters of the Congo River, which are stained by the decaying vegetation in the vast swamps of Central Africa and at flood stage push themselves far out into the Atlantic. While these dark waters cheered us with the thought that we were nearing our destination, they also reminded us that we were going into the "Dark Continent."

The Congo River is the second largest river in the world in volume of water; but its estuary is much narrower than the estuaries of many smaller rivers, being only between seven and eight miles wide at the mouth, between Banana Point on the north and Shark's Point on the south. The land along the estuary is nearly all of low elevation. The remarkable thing about the Lower Congo is the canyon through which it enters the ocean, giving its waters a depth near the mouth of nine hundred feet. This canyon extends out into the Atlantic one hundred miles, and in places reaches a depth of four thousand feet below the floor level of the ocean.

In due time we entered the mouth of the river, sailed past Banana Point, then along low-lying wooded shores and bits of grassy plains. Fetish Rock came into view on the right and soon afterwards on the left, beautiful Boma, at that time the capital of the Congo. The night was spent at Boma, discharging cargo, and the next day the journey was continued. The river above Boma is much narrower and the current swifter. Hills line both banks and in places rise to considerable height, sometimes breaking off precipitously at the water's edge.

Passing the Portuguese town of Noki on the south bank, we soon came to the Devil's Cauldron, a giant whirlpool where this huge river, which has battled its way for two hundred miles through the Crystal Mountains, after a few miles of calm forces its way through a narrow gap and hurls itself for one last mighty thrust at the foot of the mountain on the north bank. Here it has washed out a huge cauldron-shaped pool in which it seethes and swirls, then after a moment, with calm and majesty, flows on to the ocean.

As our ship nosed into the Cauldron she seemed to pause, she reeled, started to turn as though to flee from the menacing waters, then became steady and, driven by her powerful engines, slowly passed through the gap into the quieter waters beyond. The Cauldron was forgotten, for just ahead lay Matadi, the port at the head of navigation for ocean-going boats, a little less than a hundred miles from the sea.

Because of the inadequacy of the docks at Matadi, our ship anchored out in the stream and trans-shipped its cargo to lighters. Dr. A. Sims, of the American Baptist Missionary Union, who was acting as forwarding agent for the Foreign Christian Missionary Society, met us and with efficiency and dispatch soon had everything ready for our journey by rail to Léopoldville.

"Matadi" means "rock," and the town is well named, for it is built on a solid rock mountain-side that slopes up from the river. The few streets wander about in various directions to accommodate themselves to the shape of the rocky slope. Good docks, a customs house, the depot and railway shops, have since been built down by the river. A little up-river from Matadi and across on the north bank is the site of Vivi, long since deserted. This was Stanley's base station in the early days of the formation of the Congo Free State. In building the road from Vivi, Stanley's men had to blast out the rocks and so were called by the natives *"bola matadi* (rock breakers)." That term is still used over the Congo to designate any government official.

Dr. Sims was a bachelor, gruff and eccentric, yet with a warm heart. He had had long years of service in Congo. He gave us, as he did many a tenderfoot missionary, our first lesson in Congo life. It was a valuable lesson and many times during our African experiences we had reason to remember it well. The evening before we were to take an early morning train, the doctor said, "I have prepared your lunch for the two-day trip." Then

15

he enumerated the articles of food he had put in the lunch box. Among other things were two tins of sardines. I said, "Doctor, neither of us likes sardines." Quick and curt came the reply, "It isn't what you like out here, it's what you can get!"

The next morning early, with our lunch, sardines and all, we boarded the narrow-gauge, second-class passenger "coach." It was a flatcar with an awning over it and benches placed crosswise in pairs facing each other so close that one had to alternate knees and feet with the person in the opposite seat.

The night was spent at Thysville at the summit of the Crystal Mountains. It was cool but very damp. The train started early again the next morning and reached Léopoldville in late afternoon. Léopoldville is at the head of the series of rapids in which the Congo River, after having gathered all its volume, drops about eight hundred feet. Around these rapids, one of the world's greatest potential water powers, the journey was made on a train propelled by steam generated by coal mined in Europe and carried five thousand miles by ocean boats to the Congo. Of course, vast improvements have been made since then in the Congo railway, and the line will no doubt some day be electrified.

At the head of the rapids is Stanley Pool, fourteen miles wide by eighteen long, with one large and many smaller low-lying islands, around which the Congo divides into two main channels. Léopoldville, situated at the south end of the Pool, has since been made capital of the Belgian Congo. Across on the other side is Brazzaville, the capital city of French Equatorial Africa. Away across the Pool to the northward can be seen Dover Cliffs, so named because of their resemblance to the

chalk cliffs of Dover, England; but the Congo Dover
Cliffs are composed of light-colored sands, large quantities of which frequently slide into the river, endanger-
ing canoe traffic along the base of the cliffs.

After enjoying the hospitality of the Congo Balolo
Mission for a few days we boarded their steamer, the
Livingstone, to make the last lap of our journey, about
four hundred miles on up-river. Leaving Stanley Pool,
the boat traveled for about two days between beautiful
mountains, almost covered with forest and rising to a
height of about eight hundred feet. This section of the
river, one hundred twenty-five miles long, is known as
"The Channel" and varies in width from one to two
miles. About eighty-five miles from the Pool the Kwa
flows into the Congo from the right. The Kwa is a short
river but carries a tremendous volume of water. The
Kasai River, which with its several large navigable tributaries drains most of the southern part of the Congo
territory, joins with the Fini River flowing from Lake
Léopold II, and together they discharge their waters
through the Gorge de Kwa into the Congo, making the
Kwa River a swift, dangerous stream to navigate.
Beyond the mouth of the Kwa the mountains decrease
in height and are a considerable distance back from the
river.

In the next day's steaming, beyond the Kwa we passed
two Protestant mission stations on the right bank of the
river, Tshumbiri of the American Baptist Foreign Missionary Society, and Bolobo of the Baptist Missionary
Society of Great Britain. Tshumbiri has since become
a station of the B.M.S. Between these stations the river
widens, and one begins the journey among wooded islands of which the Congo has more than four thousand,

some fifty of them over ten miles in length. The two longest islands, Esumba and Nsumbu, are thirty and fifty miles long, respectively.

Beyond Bolobo the patches of open prairie disappear and islands and mainland are alike covered with the densest kind of forest. Great trees are woven together with almost every conceivable kind of vine and brush. All the waterways are lined with beautiful green draperies hanging down from the trees with their vine fringes trailing in the water. It is beautiful but monotonous. One could take a picture in one place and it would fit just as well in ten thousand other places. Yet as appreciation for the jungle grows, one observes infinite variety and constant change from month to month with the varying seasons.

It was flood-time on the Congo, so we saw but little of the animal life on this first trip. When the water was low, in those years before steamer traffic became so abundant on the river, one could see the hippopotami in many places playing around in the shallow water or basking in the sunshine on the sand-banks. And crocodiles would sometimes be lined up in rows taking their siestas on the sandy beds that rise above the water— man-eating crocodiles that look as if they might eat a person at one meal and still be hungry. Every year they do get many natives who are venturesome enough to go in swimming in the Congo. Many and gruesome are the stories told of victims carried away screaming for help, of half-eaten bodies found later, or of the crunching of bones heard by a searching party that comes upon the crocodile unawares as he is enjoying his meal. A crocodile killed at one mission station had eleven pairs of anklets and bracelets in its stomach.

Even though the water was high, we saw a few crocodiles and by a lucky shot I succeeded in killing one asleep on the main bank of the river. Some of the crew went ashore in a canoe we were towing alongside and brought the crocodile out to the steamer. The rest of that day the natives were busy cutting it up, cooking it in their clay pots on the lower deck, and having a big feast of crocodile meat.

The next day our long trip from Portland, Oregon, to Central Congo came to an end right where the river crosses the Equator. There on the right bank, on a high piece of land that commands a magnificent view of the Congo River, is beautiful Bolenge, the oldest station of the Disciples of Christ Congo Mission. As it came into view that day, its lawns and well-kept paths lined with palms and orange trees afforded a pleasant relief from the monotony of the jungle wall along the river.

As soon as the people of Bolenge village had time to size us up, they came to give us our African names. Among the Bankundo, Bokecu and Mboyo are names frequently given to twins. Mrs. Dye, who had served ten years in Africa and was at that time in America, had been given the name "Mboyo." The natives thought Mrs. Moon resembled her a great deal, so they called her "Bokecu." They had heard about the shooting of the crocodile, so they named me "Ikoko," after a native who had quite a reputation in that district for being a great hunter.

Our landing at Bolenge and the receiving of our African names brought to an end our honeymoon trip. What we had expected to last a few days and take us a few hundred miles had stretched out into months, touched three continents, and covered about twelve thousand miles.

I suppose if we had returned immediately to America I would have said, "I saw Congo," and would never have realized how little I had actually seen. Africa keeps its secrets well hidden from the casual traveler. It is only through years of patient, loving service for and with the Congo people that they open to the outsider the wonders of their forest homes and the innermost secrets of their lives. It is this Congoland as it was gradually unfolded to me during fifteen years that I want to share with you in the succeeding chapters.

PART ONE

RIVER AND JUNGLE TRAIL

STEAMBOAT ON THE CONGO

THE WHOLE INTERIOR of the Congo Basin was once a vast inland sea. The water broke through the mountains to the westward, drained the sea and formed the great Congo River system. These great waterways reach out into every part of the Belgian Congo. They were the natural and until recently almost the only means of communication and transportation. And until the coming of steamboats, dugout canoes were the only vessels that plied these waters. They were the trade routes for the native merchants, and their word for "profit" or "gain" comes from the root word meaning "to paddle a canoe."

At first the missionaries were dependent on this method of travel. It was very slow and dangerous. There was danger from the hot tropical sun, danger from the *tsetse*

flies that carry the sleeping sickness, danger from hidden
snags and from crocodiles and hippopotami that sometimes attack canoes. It was soon evident as the mission
work grew that some safer and faster method of travel
must be provided. A steamboat seemed to be the only
answer.

Just as this need for a steamboat in our mission became
most pressing Dr. and Mrs. Royal J. Dye came home to
America for their furlough. In June, 1908, in one of her
addresses at the Oregon state convention, Mrs. Dye told
of the difficulties and dangers of canoe travel along the
hundreds of miles of waterways to reach our growing
missionary work, and showed the great need of a steamboat. When she finished, David Errett, the president of
the convention, stood up and said, "Why not raise the
money right here in Oregon for that boat and call it 'The
Oregon'?" A young man, James Blood, said: "I have
saved a little money on which to go to school. I will give
that to start the fund." The convention was enthusiastic.
Committees were appointed. The churches of the state
were visited and the money was raised.

When word reached Bolenge that the mission was to
have a steamboat, the native Christians exclaimed,
"Nsang'ea ndoci (good news)," and that became the
Congo name for the *Oregon*. Since that is their translation of the word for "gospel" it was quite appropriate,
for it was certainly a gospel ship.

The S.S. *Oregon* was built by Tom Rees and Sons,
shipbuilders in Pittsburgh, Pennsylvania. It was completed and temporarily bolted together and dedicated in
the shipyard during the Centennial Convention of the
Disciples of Christ in October, 1909. After the dedica-
tion it was taken apart and shipped in small packages to

Congo where it had to be sent by the small, narrow-gauge railway around the rapids on the Lower Congo.

Mrs. Moon and I had been in the Congo a little more than a year when the pile of material that was to be the *Oregon* arrived. At Kinshasa, now East Lépoldville, on Stanley Pool at the head of the rapids, the British Baptist Mission Society had a station with a well-equipped machine shop and two steamers of their own. They graciously granted us permission to reassemble the *Oregon* on their beach. It was especially advantageous to us, for a spur of the little railway ran out to their station and we could unload our material there.

The head of the railway is four hundred miles down-river from our station at Bolenge. Mr. Robert S. Wilson, a graduate of The College of the Bible, Lexington, Kentucky, whose boat experience had been as a deep-sea sailor, and I, whose steamboat experience had been as a passenger on the Columbia River steamers, were asked to go down to Kinshasa, receive the material, and make a boat out of it. We pooled our ignorance and undertook the job.

The *Oregon* was a shallow-draught, stern-wheel river steamer, with eighteen-foot beam and ninety feet over-all in length. The hull and lower deck were steel. The frame was put together with one-half- and three-quarter-inch hot rivets, and the plates double-riveted with three-eighths-inch cold rivets. It took about twenty thousand rivets for the hull. These were put in by hand by the native crew we brought down from Bolenge. They had never seen a rivet hammer or a dolly-bar until we put them in their hands and showed them their use.

We had a good set of blue-prints which fortunately we were able to read. We built a cradle according to specifications and on June 4, 1910, began the work of putting the boat together. We lived in the homes of the two British missionary families in charge of the station, the John Howells and the Alfred Stonelakes. A little ceremony was held as we started work and we asked Mrs. Howell, wife of the senior missionary, to put in the first bolt. That day we made good progress and by quitting time had bolted in place almost the full set of ribs. It looked as if we had about built a boat in a day. Mr. Howell wrote to a friend the next day and said, "If you want a boat built while you wait, call on Moon and Wilson."

The river was high when we began and we built the cradle as close to the water as we could work. By the time the hull was completed the water had receded so that our launchways had to be seventy feet long.

We had set the launching for ten o'clock on a certain day and had invited in groups of French, Belgian, and British friends. The evening before the day set for the launching, Mr. Stonelake came down to see how we were getting on. He noted that the hull was still resting on the blocks and not on the launchways. He asked, "When are you going to let it down on the ways?" I replied, "In the morning." "You'd better not wait," he warned. "It will take you longer than you think. You will have the folks here waiting and not be ready. It took us three days to let our boat down on the ways."

I spoke with assurance. "The jacks are all set, ready by a turn to take the weight, and we can slip the blocks out and let it down. I'll risk it in the morning." We always worked an hour before breakfast. The next morning when the missionary in company with a friend came to call us to breakfast, the boat was on the ways ready to slide in as soon as the ropes were cut. He turned to his friend and said, "These Americans don't claim to be engineers, but somehow they do get things done."

We greased the launchways with home-made soft soap which we had brought down river for that purpose. After a fitting service we cut the ropes and the boat slid in, with Wilson standing on deck. The launching was perfect. Mr. Howell, who had spent many years in missionary service and had seen the launching of almost every boat that had been built on the Congo, complimented us: "You are to be congratulated. That was the most perfect launching that has ever taken place on the Congo River."

After the launching, the boiler and machinery had to be set and the upper deck and cabins built. By November, we had made a trial run and were loaded with cargo for our first trip up river. Wilson acted as captain and I as engineer. He was looking after the native pilots and I was training engineers and firemen to take charge below. The trip was made without mishap, and it was a happy day at Bolenge when the *Oregon*'s deep, three-toned whistle first announced its approach. After that, Mr. Wilson made one trip down river and back with the *Oregon*. During the trip he injured his leg and had to return to America. That left me in sole charge of the *Oregon* for some years.

On my first trip up river I was breaking in a new steersman. I stood by him all the first day. By the second day he seemed to be getting along all right, so I slipped down to see how the machinery was working. While down there I looked out and saw that we were heading right into the forest-lined bank. I got up to the wheel in time to ease the shock, so but little damage was done. After a year or two we had a number of well-trained men for each responsible position on the boat.

In those early years there were few places where wood could be purchased, and every steamboat had to carry enough men to cut wood after running hours to last the next day. Through the years most of the crew on the *Oregon* were Christians. Non-Christians seldom worked on the boat for long before they wanted to be baptized.

W. H. Edwards, a sturdy Scotsman and a well-trained engineer, joined our mission after serving one term with the Congo Balolo Mission, the British mission society working in the Congo. When he returned from furlough in 1917, he was given full charge of the S.S. *Oregon*. A young fellow named John Inkima, who had been sold into slavery when a baby and was later redeemed by one of the British missionaries on the station where Mr. Edwards had been located, came and asked for work on the *Oregon*. As he had worked some in the steamer shop for the other mission, he was made assistant engineer. Later he became first engineer. The whole mission was impressed with this fine, dependable Christian young man. When the time came that we felt the steamer should be put entirely in charge of a native crew, John was the unanimous choice for captain. He was taken up to the upper deck and taught to navigate. When he was proficient the steamer was turned over to him. For nearly three decades John had full charge of the *Oregon* and no one ever had reason to regret his choice as captain.

If you were a passenger on the S.S. *Oregon* the first thing you would hear in the morning would be Captain John calling the fireman. When the steam pressure was about high enough for starting, a few taps of the ship's bell called the crew to an early morning prayer service. John led them in singing a hymn, read a passage of Scripture, exhorted them in a few words, then one or more fervent prayers closed the service. The members of the crew took their places and the day's run began. Passengers had time for another good nap before time for breakfast. If you were acquainted with the dark background of heathenism from which these Africans had so recently come you would be deeply stirred as you listened to the early morning prayer meeting.

One can hardly think of missions in Equatorial Congo without thinking of the S.S. *Oregon* that for nearly forty years carried Christian workers up and down the Congo and its tributaries. And one cannot think of the *Oregon* apart from Captain John. Trading companies and the government tried many times by the offer of a large salary to entice John to leave the mission and take charge of one of their boats, but he always said he owed too much to the mission ever to leave it.

Time brings change. Automobile roads are being opened up and there is now some air service between the larger centers in Congo. More rapid transportation is available than by water. Moreover, the *Oregon* finally reached a state when the cost of repairs were too great to pay to keep it in service. So it was sold to a commercial company. The last trip was made in service of the mission. Captain John, now grown old in service, blew the whistle for the last time and stepped ashore. Thus ended a most notable active career of a first generation Christian life that puts to shame many of us who have generations of Christianity behind us.

No other single agency has surpassed the *Oregon* in

the value of the service rendered to the cause of Christian missions in the Congo. It was a cargo boat for transporting mission supplies, a passenger boat for carrying missionaries and native Christian workers to and from fields of labor, a hospital ship to take doctors and medical supplies to the sick or to bring the sick and injured to our hospitals. Besides its great service to the native population and to missionaries, many white traders and government officials have reason to remember the *Oregon* with grateful hearts and to offer a prayer in behalf of those in America who made the boat possible and financed its running through the years.

The *Oregon* was a great little ship, on one of the world's greatest systems of water highways, engaged in the greatest possible work any boat could be called upon to do.

CHAPTER II

THE GAME TRAIL

 N ZALA (MEAT HUNGER)"
is one of the most widely
used words throughout Bantu
Africa, and probably no expression is more frequently
heard than *"Njobwa la nzala
(I am dying from meat hunger)."* Both along the rivers
and in the hinterland I have
been urged over and over again by the Congo people to
kill meat for them. In all the hunting I did I never knew
of an ounce of meat going to waste.

Fishing and hunting by the natives are seasonal, and
since they have no adequate method of preserving meat
the supply is soon finished and there are long periods of
shortage. Most of the hunting done by missionaries is
in response to the cry of hunger rather than for the mere
joy of the sport.

During the first few weeks after arriving at Bolenge

31

I Saw Congo

I often looked with longing eyes at the great forest-lined shores across the river. Imagine my thrill when Dr. Charles Widdowson, our station doctor, and Dr. Louis Jaggard, who was taking a little rest away from his station at Longa, proposed a few days' hunting trip. There was need for a supply of smoked meat for the mission workmen and for the orphans, but I have always had a suspicion that the chief incentive back of that hunting trip was a curiosity on the part of the doctors to know just how the new missionary with his fifty-calibre Winchester would behave when he faced some of Africa's big game for the first time.

All things were made ready the evening before. About two o'clock in the morning we set forth in two large canoes for the low-lying peninsula between the Congo and the Ubangi River which flows into it from the north. The hunting ground chosen was probably some thirty or forty miles distant and our course lay across the river, here about seven miles wide, then down along the north bank. We had some twelve or fifteen native paddlers in each canoe. In the canoe in which I was riding was a *lokoli,* the native drum which serves as the chief means of native communication in Congo. A *lokoli* is carried on canoe journeys to beat a steady rhythm to which the men dip their paddles and sing their canoe songs. The drum is also used to communicate with villages along the way.

We soon crossed the seven-mile expanse of the Congo at the Equator and began the descent with the swift current along the north bank. The drummer suddenly stopped his steady rhythm and began to send out a message. After finishing his broadcasting, he again resumed the steady, rhythmic beat for the paddlers. When we had journeyed on for some miles the canoe slowed down and drew near to land. The man at the drum spoke. A woman standing on shore in the darkness answered and handed him a bundle and we passed on. Then it was all explained to me. While we were yet miles away this drummer had sent word to his sister living in that village, that he was passing by. She received the message, prepared him some food, tied it up in a banana leaf, and handed it to him as we passed. That is Congo "curb service."

The hunt was a success, every man bringing down a fair share of the game. We shot several hippopotami, a buffalo, and some smaller game, and had tons of meat smoking at one time. We returned to the station after some days, tired and sleepy and nearly eaten up by mosquitoes in spite of the protection of our mosquito nets. My wife insisted that the whole party smelled like half-smoked, over-ripe meat. Be that as it may, the native force of the mission had many a good meal of the meat we brought back.

Hippopotami have their favorite haunts and are sometimes found in considerable numbers in these places. I have seen twenty or thirty playing in shallow water in late afternoon. They have slept on the sand-banks or lazily wallowed around in the water during the heat of the day, but evening is their play time. There is then a glorious plunging and splashing, swimming and diving, spouting and snorting. The hippos are boisterous when at play and laugh with their mouths wide open. As night falls they scatter out in the feeding grounds along the waterways.

The hippopotamus is not vicious as a rule but often resents being disturbed in his favorite haunts. In such places canoes are frequently upset or destroyed by them and sometimes unfortunate victims are crushed between their gigantic jaws or pierced through with their tusks. Hippopotami are not carnivorous, and after crushing their victims they leave them.

Opposite Bolenge station on the north bank of the river is a small village called Bakanga. There is always an abundance of game to be found on that side of the river: buffalo, hippopotami, elephants, wild hogs, and also chimpanzees, leopards, and crocodiles. Dr. William A. Frymire, our surgeon of Lotumbe mission station, and I were once at Bakanga village when elephants spent the night in the gardens just back of the row of native houses. At daylight we went out to try our luck at getting one of them. They had left the gardens, but we followed them into the forest and soon overtook them. We shot and wounded the big bull of the herd but before we could get him down he started straight back from the river into the deep forest.

We followed the wounded elephant hour after hour, hoping to get another shot. We had as a guide a small-sized man, not a member of the pigmy tribe, but no larger than many of them. He led the way and we followed, through thorny thickets and across dismal swamps. Where the water was over our heads we clung to the brush and clawed our way along, holding our guns high above our heads to keep them dry. Fortunately, we did not meet the elephant in one of these places. Just as we started into the edge of one swamp our guide said, "Wait a bit." He slipped off to one side and when I looked again he was standing with his spear thrust through a small crocodile about six feet long and was reaching for the big knife which he carried in his belt, to kill it. It was soon done. The crocodile was given to one of the other natives in our party to carry, and we were off again.

At one time we plunged right into the midst of a drove of wild hogs that scattered in every direction. We did not want to shoot lest we might be near the wounded elephant and would frighten it again. After pausing for a few moments, I noticed that our guide was empty-handed. "Where is your spear?" I asked. "In the hog," he replied. Following a trail of blood for fifty yards, we found the hog dead, with the spear-head buried in it, the shaft broken off.

It was after midday when we finally caught up with our elephant. The brush was so thick that we were unable to get a good shot and he was off again. We then gave up the chase, for we knew that it would be dark before we could get back and we were not prepared to spend the night in the jungle. We hoped to take up the chase the next day and see it through. They were anxious about us back at the village and a party with lights came out considerable distance into the jungle to meet us. It was probably well for us that they did, for it was getting too dark to follow the trail we had made that morning.

When we arrived at the village we found messengers from the station calling the doctor back immediately. So in spite of the ethics of hunting, one law of which is never to leave a wounded animal, we were unable to take up the trail again. About ten days later we received word that the villagers in the area where we had been had found a dead elephant. I had told them before leaving that if they found the elephant it was theirs.

As there was always great attraction for me in a good hunting ground, it is not surprising that another occasion found me at the village of Bakanga. This time I was accompanied by Dr. Jaggard. We spent the night on board the S.S. *Oregon*. Early the next morning we paddled in a small canoe a few miles up the river. Leaving the canoe, we soon took up the trail of a mother elephant and her baby. We did not want them, but followed, thinking they might lead us to the herd where we could get a larger tusker. In the heavy forest the herds are small, usually not over five or six animals. The baby tracks were just little round holes punched in the soft marshy ground. After some time we overtook the two animals, and approaching very cautiously we were able to get within a few yards of them. The mother was feeding on the leaves of the trees and the baby was standing by her side. My native gun-bearer whispered in my ear, "Shoot the mother and let us capture the baby." As the Belgian colonial law forbids the shooting of female elephants, except in self-defense, I shook my head.

Just then we heard another elephant off to our right. Slipping over that way, we could see it through the brush at a distance of about eighty yards. It was facing toward us. It had small tusks not over three feet long. My gun-bearer, to whom I had given permission to shoot that day, whispered, "Shall we shoot?" Disappointed that it was not a big tusker, I spoke right out, "No, it's too small!"

When the elephant heard my voice it extended its huge ears and charged. Our first volley checked it, but even the second failed to bring it down. Before we could shoot again, another elephant, which we had not seen, charged toward us. As it neared we saw it was going to pass within a few steps so we held our fire. When it was directly opposite, we aimed for the heart and killed it. We then turned our attention to the first one, which was still standing; we brought it down. Unfortunately, they were both females and did not have large tusks, but we knew that many a hungry native would be made happy by sharing in the meat.

The African elephant is much larger than the Indian elephants which one sees in circuses. The Indian elephants attain a height of from seven to nine feet, while a full-grown African elephant will attain a height of twelve feet and will extend its huge ears, as it does when charging, as much as twelve feet from tip to tip.

It was late in the evening when we returned to the steamer at Bakanga. Immediately upon our arrival at the village, one of the men in our party went to the big drum and began to broadcast the success of the day's hunt. Mrs. Moon was back at the mission station seven miles away, just sitting down to the evening meal. A native boy was bringing in the service from the kitchen when he stopped in the middle of the floor and stood like a statue. Mrs. Moon wondered at his pose, but said nothing. Presently he smiled and said, "Mr. Moon has killed two elephants." He started on toward the table but stopped, as the message was being repeated. After her attention had been called to it, Mrs. Moon noticed that the drum was beating over at Bakanga. When the message was finished, the boy said, "Yes, he has killed two elephants and is coming home tomorrow evening."

That was according to our plan, for we expected to go into the jungle the next morning to cut up the elephants and carry the meat out to the boat. This would be an all-day job. The next evening when we returned to the station we learned that people within a radius of ten to twelve miles had heard the message, and many were there to greet the hunters and share in the spoils.

In 1916, I helped make a missionary survey of the District of the Ubangi. One day the meat supply for our carriers was getting low. Securing a guide from the village where we were encamped, I started out to bring back whatever kind of game we might find. This was an open country with scattered patches of woodland. Like most of tropical Africa, it was dotted with huge anthills, large clay mounds built up by the white ants (termites) often to a height of fifteen feet or more. The grass was higher than our heads, so at short intervals the guide would climb an anthill and look for game. He had climbed a number without success, but finally I saw him duck out of sight as he looked away toward the north. When he came down he said, *"Mbolo!"* I knew hardly a word of his language, so I climbed the anthill to find out what *"mbolo"* meant. There, about one hundred fifty yards away, stood a lone buffalo bull.

These lone bulls may be animals that have been whipped out of the herd and therefore are in an ugly mood and are very dangerous. Not wishing to try a shot at that distance, especially since the buffalo was facing from me, I slipped up nearer and climbed another anthill within fifty yards of him. He had either heard or scented me, for as I put my head above the hill he was looking me square in the face. I was carrying a sporting model of the .30 U.S.G. rifle, which is a little light for buffalo, and I had only five cartridges to my name. These buffalo have a small brain and a very hard bone in the front of the head, sloping well back. This makes a head shot uncertain. I immediately decided to wait until he turned to flee or charged. Being on an anthill about fifteen feet high, I figured I had somewhat the advantage in case of a charge. So Mr. Buffalo and I stood there, staring each other straight in the eyes. It must have been but a few moments, although it seemed like a very long time. Finally I could see that he was getting nervous. He flicked one ear, then the other, then both together; then he whirled to run. But before he made the first jump I sent a ball that broke his shoulder. This old bull was not the finest beef in the world, but our carriers were glad to get it. They all enjoyed a good feed that day and smoked the surplus to carry along as we continued our journey.

Many are the tales of African hunters who have lost their lives hunting the buffalo. A wounded buffalo is very dangerous, for even though it may run when shot, you can usually count on its lying in wait for you as soon as it finds cover, from which it charges its pursuers with deadly certainty. Many hunters have been killed by carelessly coming up to a fallen buffalo, especially one that has been shot in the head. Often they are only stunned and they revive in a very bad humor. .

I went out one day, against my judgment, with four other men for a buffalo hunt. I never liked to go hunting with a crowd. Two hunters who understand each other may be an aid to greater safety, but more than two only increases the danger. We soon located a small herd of about twenty buffalo in a patch of forest of perhaps an acre. The five of us were advancing abreast a few rods apart. I occupied the center position. We began to flank this patch of forest, when suddenly the herd ran off in front of us. When they reached the summit of a little ridge about one hundred yards away, they whirled in unison and lined up facing us like a well-drilled company of cavalry. It looked as if we were in for some excitement. The herd stood perfectly still while the bull leader charged for the end man to my right. Somebody fired and missed. As the buffalo neared the man it was charging, it was nearly broadside to me and by a lucky shoulder shot I brought it down. When the leader fell, to our great relief the rest of the herd turned and fled.

The following amusing incident was told me by A. E. Scrivener of the Baptist mission station at Bolobo. Some of the natives had been borrowing his gun with which to hunt, and being very fond of monkeys and knowing that Mr. Scrivener would not eat them, they repeatedly brought in nothing else, so that they alone profited by the hunt. One day when they came for the gun, Mr. Scrivener refused, saying, "You can't have it, for you never bring in any meat that I care to eat." They promised faithfully that they would bring him some choice meat if he would only let them have the gun once more. He agreed and three of them started out.

Before long they brought down a buffalo. They could not carry it in, so they cut off the tail and sent one man back to the station with this evidence of success, to call sufficient workmen to carry in the buffalo. The other two men sat down on the beast to wait. The messenger had not been gone long when the buffalo gave a snort, sprang to its feet, and fled. When the party arrived all they found was two very frightened natives up a tree. All they had of that buffalo was oxtail soup.

As far as my observations have gone, the monkey seems to be universally hunted and used for food in the Congo. One day I shot a large white monkey from the deck of our steamer. Its skin and hair were white and its face freckled. It was an uncanny thing to look at, so much so that the Ba-Nkundo people, of whom most of the crew consisted, refused to eat it. In fact, the first man to go ashore to get the monkey came back without it. There were, however, some men of the Ngombe tribe who were glad to get it. The monkey was in company with some *ngila,* a coal-black species of monkey which it resembled in every respect except color. I concluded that it must have been an albino *ngila.*

Among the numerous kinds of monkeys found in the Congo are two species that have no thumbs, known as the *jibuka* and the *jafe.* The former is a large monkey with white hair about the neck that from the front resembles a long white beard. The *jafe* has very beautiful red fur. One day while hunting I shot a *jafe.* The natives told me that the way to kill them was to call out when you see one, *"Jafe* has only eight fingers." The monkey would feel so humiliated because he has no thumbs that he would sit perfectly still and let you shoot him!

During the early days of our work at Mondombe station, one morning before daylight the big "radio" drum in the chief's compound was kept going for some time. Then smaller drums from each section of the town answered. As soon as some of our employees came to the mission house, I asked them what it was all about. They informed me that a leopard had killed five of the chief's goats and he was calling the hunters together to try to get the culprit. I wanted to get into the hunt, but we were housed in such miserable quarters that instead I went with the workmen down by the river to work on the new house we were building. We were therefore about a mile and a half from the chief's place. But we knew everything that went on that day, for a man stood at the drum and broadcast every phase of the hunt, just as they do big ball games in other countries.

Shortly after we started to work, the drum beat and the workmen interpreting for me said, "They have tracked the leopard and found where it is hiding in the brush." There was near the chief's place a patch of second-growth brush of perhaps one acre. They tracked the leopard and soon found where it had entered this patch of brush. When after careful investigation they found no tracks leading away they knew the leopard was hiding within.

When the drum beat again we learned that they had surrounded this brush with their hunting nets and stationed a man with a spear every few yards to guard the net and keep the leopard inside. Later we received the message that they had cut a path through the center and stretched another net, thus enclosing the leopard in half the original plot of ground. Again the drum beat and the message was that the leopard had tried to escape but was met by the spearmen at the net and that he had returned to the center of the brush. Thus it went on all forenoon. After lunch I was getting the fever so strongly that I could not stay away longer, so I took my high-power rifle and went out.

The hunters had gradually cut down the plot where the leopard was hiding until it was not more than one-sixth of an acre. Inside the net, down on hands and knees were the chief and three of his best hunters, with some spears and knives and one old muzzle-loading gun, the only kind the natives were permitted to own. I got inside with them and went down on my knees, with my rifle ready to use. The method was to cut away a small bit of brush, crawl in a little way, and look very carefully in every direction for the object of our hunt. We spent most of the time looking. I had been there some time and we had made some progress, when the chief said to me, *"Bondele* (white man), the men guarding the net are afraid of your rifle and are leaving the net unguarded." I hated to quit, but fearing lest I might be the cause of letting the leopard escape, I left and went back to work again a mile and a half away.

The messages kept coming. About four o'clock the workmen interpreted a longer message than usual, which said, "They have killed the leopard, but the leopard has nearly killed two men who were inside the net." Their names, Iyambe and Boloma, were also broadcast so we knew who the unfortunate ones were. With medical aid we were able to save the men who had been mauled by the animal, though they were left crippled. It may be a good thing for me that I was ruled out of the game!

CHAPTER III

SNAKES, FISH, INSECTS

S NAKES? Yes, Congo has them, a great many different kinds. But the surprise of my Congo experience was the comparatively few snakes one sees. Before going to Africa I pictured great serpents draped down from the limbs of every tree in the forest. I have actually seen more snakes, though perhaps not so dangerous, in one day in places in America than I ever saw in any six months in the Congo. On one trip of one hundred days which took us afoot over plains and jungle trail and along small streams in canoes, I saw only three snakes. In the clearings around villages or mission stations, one will see more, but not many.

Python are found with their tremendous capacity for swallowing dogs, goats, and sometimes even people. Sir Harry Johnston in *George Grenfell and the Congo* gives

45

an extract from a letter of the Rev. Hunter Reid in
which Mr. Reid tells of shooting a python twenty-five
feet long which held in its grip at the time two native
men. ". . . the stomach of the snake contained not less
than one peck of brass, copper, and iron rings, such as
natives wear on the arms and legs . . . A snake that
size would swallow an antelope as large as a cow, horns
and all." [1]

All over the Central Congo Basin the natives told me
of a snake which they call "*jibate*," that "throws poisonous missiles," hurling them with deadly accuracy fifteen
or twenty feet. One man told me that they would always throw at some bright object. He said, "If you
are carrying a gun with some bright metal parts, just
hold the gun off to one side and you can hear the missiles
strike the metal one at a time. When the snake has
hurled all its missiles it is harmless, but if you do not kill
it, after you are gone it will gather them up to use
again." I never put any stock in the story, for I soon
found that while the children of the jungle have a wonderful general knowledge of animal life, their observations are made with far from scientific accuracy.

At Mondombe mission station we had as sentry a
Batswa. The Batswa are a small people and are frequently referred to as pigmies. They are probably the
keenest woodsmen of all Central Congo peoples. One
day as I returned from work this sentry met me, and
pointing to an ugly serpent as large as my forearm and
about five feet long, with a broad head, he said, "There
is one of those serpents that you say do not exist." I

---

[1] Used by permission of the publisher, Appleton-Century-Crofts, Inc.

replied, "Yes, there is a snake; but I have not seen it throw anything yet."

Then I examined the head and found one fang over an inch long. However, the fang that should have been opposite was gone. Buried under the remaining fang, and where the missing one had been, were several others in various stages of development. I could see that the snake had swallowed something, so I had it cut open and found a large species of rat. Buried full depth in the side of the rat was the missing fang. The natives gave a triumphant "We told you so." I think likely the fangs are left in the game when the snake strikes in the usual way, but one would have to prove that to the natives. I have been informed by others that there are irregular missiles that are actually thrown by the *jibate,* but that they do not throw their fangs.

I asked the sentry where he killed the snake. This is the way he told it: "I was going along the path that leads across the swamp when I heard two little squirrels laughing. I passed on and then I began to wonder what they were laughing at. I said to myself, 'They wouldn't be laughing for nothing.' So I went back and watched them for a while and noticed that they kept looking in a certain direction. I slipped over there and found this *jibate* asleep. I got a club and hit it, *piau-piau-piau,* and here it is." Then the natives carried snake, rat, and all out to the village to have a feast.

A native woman dressed only in a banana leaf was going along the broad station path one day when she saw a serpent six feet long, of a deadly poisonous variety, just disappearing into the brush at the side of the path. She could not bear to see this choice bit of meat slipping away, so grabbed it by the tail and threw it back into the path. She had nothing with which to kill it, but one of our workmen who was passing with a club in his hand soon dealt the fatal blow. Then very gallantly he cut off the head and gave it to the woman for her share of the meat, keeping the rest for his share. She was not at all pleased. She called her husband and they went to the workman, who refused any other division. As usual when no agreement could be reached, they soon appeared before me, bringing the two pieces of the snake. When I heard the story I was convinced that the woman had not had a square deal, so I made a more equitable division and all went away happy to prepare the evening meal.

There are many fish in the Congo waters. When the water is high, great quantities of small fish like sardines are caught in bamboo cone-shaped traps anchored in the swift water at rocky points. At low water many larger fish are caught in seines woven out of native-made cord. Large channel catfish are sometimes caught on hooks and lines. Large fish are also speared in the heavy grass near shore. Another kind of fishing is that done in the swamps. When the water recedes after the floods, it leaves thousands of fish entrapped in shallow pools. The natives close the outlets of many swamps with closely woven bamboo fencing, so as to let the water out but keep the fish in. When the pools are nearly drained, the water is bailed out and poured through baskets. The fish are either caught in the baskets or picked up out of the mud.

The open river fishing is done by the men, but much of the swamp fishing is the work of the women. In the days of inter-tribal warfare, when the women were fishing in the swamps was a favorite time for the enemy to swoop down and carry them away. Out of this grew one of the native proverbs: *"Bonjemba aobwa nd'etumba ey' okeji lae?* (Why should the single man die in the fight in the swamp?)"* (He has no wife, therefore nothing at stake; why then should he jeopardize himself by going out to fight in the swamp?)

Ants, ants, ants, multitudinous and indescribable—where shall I begin to tell about them? There is a little red ant that seems almost as pervasive as the atmosphere. Every tiny little nook and crevice is their home. One of their favorite hiding places is inside cameras. It is a common experience to rush in and pick up your camera to get some rare picture, only to find it filled with these ants and their tiny white eggs. If you try to brush them out, the tiny eggs are crushed and your camera is left in a mess. About the only thing you can do is to forego taking the picture and carefully open up the camera and place it in the hot sun. The ants will then remove all the eggs, doing a much better job than you could.

It is a constant fight to keep ants out of food cupboards and off of dining-tables. Standing the legs of cupboards and tables in pans of water or crude carbolic acid, or insulating the legs with bichloride tape, are methods used to keep them out of food. Even then, they are constantly getting by. If a chair is left touching an overhanging tablecloth they soon find it. If a cobweb falls across the cup in which the cupboard leg stands, that is bridge enough for them and they soon are swarming over the food. These ants are sometimes spoken of as "the kind that everybody eats."

Over against the ants that everybody eats, are the ants that eat everybody. The army ants, or driver ants, as they are sometimes called, will eat anything in the world in the way of meat, living or dead. There is not an animal in the jungle, so far as I know, except the ant-eater, that is not afraid of them. In the open, almost any animal can get away from them; but if enclosed in a room or pen, dog, sheep, goat, or any other creature is soon devoured. A bird in a room is quickly captured. After one or two ants get hold of it, it flutters about in pain and every time it touches wall, floor, or ceiling where the ants are swarming more lay hold on it. They hang on with bulldog tenacity until the bird falls helplessly to the floor.

The army ants are of medium size, are dark red in color, and have no eyes, working entirely by scent. There are two classes, the workers and the warriors. The warriors are much larger than the workers and have large black mandibles. When they take hold, you can pull them in two before they will let loose. The army ants usually travel in runways one and a half or two inches wide. If their path lies across an open roadway it is guarded on each side by a line of soldiers facing outward, with mandibles raised. If you stamp your foot within three or four feet of them they all march forward to find the cause of the disturbance. When disturbed very much they call enough soldiers to form a living tunnel, by locking themselves together, under which the workers pass to and fro, entirely hidden from view. The narrow runways are connecting paths between their nesting place and their feeding ground. As they advance, they scatter out over considerable territory, capturing and killing and carrying back to the nest.

When driver ants come into a house, which they do occasionally, every living creature—rat, bat, or insect—

gets out or they take it out. Every house in Africa needs such a cleaning periodically, so when they come in the human occupants leave and let them have their way. They will finish in two or three hours. It is sometimes inconvenient when they come at night, which time they usually choose. However, if one has a good mosquito net, well tucked in, he is perfectly safe, for they never cut through.

Once on a long missionary exploration trip William H. Holder and I spent the night in a new village. When natives move a village in Congo, it is customary to carry some pieces of thatched roofing from their old houses and set them up for temporary shelters until their new houses are ready. Holder and I stayed in a shelter which consisted of two such pieces for a roof and two more for walls, with one end partly closed. It was little wider than our two army cots, so our mosquito nets hung against the thatched walls.

During the night I heard something crawling in the dry thatching at the end of my bed, and fearing that it might be a serpent, I reached for the candle which it is customary to keep under the pillow so one can have a light without raising the net. It was not there, and I remembered that I had left it and the matches on the trunk at the head of the cot. I raised the net and reached for the candle, but before I could pick it up I knew what was happening, for a perfect shower of driver ants rained down on my arms and bald head. I closed the net as quickly as possible, but not before hundreds of ants were inside. I called, "Bill, are you all right?" He sleepily answered, "Yes, what's the matter?" "Strike a light," I said. "My bed is full of drivers."

It was safer to stay under the net and wage war on

those within, for outside it would have been worse. Bill lay there and enjoyed my predicament until I had them pretty well killed off. Then the ants began to rain down on him through a hole which he had forgotten in the top of his net. It was my turn to laugh.

In the morning the ants were feeding somewhere beyond our shelter and had settled down to two narrow runways underneath our cots. By stepping out carefully so as not to disturb them, we had no more trouble. When I took the blankets off my cot I found roaches, crickets, centipedes, and scorpions that had squeezed in there to seek refuge from the invading army. What had awakened me in the first place was the lizards fleeing from the ants in the dry thatching.

The *"mpono"* is a small black ant with a poisonous bite. These ants are the only things I know, except a barrage of fire, that will turn back an army of driver ants. One morning on the station path I saw some white ants (termites) pouring from a hole and marching down the path. That was unusual, for they seldom come out into the light. Investigating, I found that the *mpono* had gone into their hole through another opening and routed them. A little way down the path, some driver ants met the fleeing white ants and began to kill them. I saw that the helpless white ants with the drivers in front and the *mpono* behind would soon be exterminated and was waiting for the battle royal when the drivers and *mpono* should meet. Just then a last impatient call for breakfast came. It was one of those calls when first and middle names are sounded in full and you know it is time to move. When I returned after breakfast, the battle was over and an old hen was calmly picking up the casualties.

The little termites, commonly called white ants, abound everywhere in the Congo. They are so soft one can hardly touch them without crushing them, and yet houses and trees fall before them and Central Africa is studded with solid clay mounds from ten feet to twenty feet high, the work of these tiny creatures. They do not attack living trees or plants, but make short work of them when dead. A few trees they do not eat, not because the wood is too hard, but because they do not like them. They never work in the open, but bore into the interior or cover the object over with a thin layer of clay and then crawl between the clay and the wood or other objects on which they are working.

One morning after sleeping in a native hut built on top of an anthill, I found my shoes entirely covered with a thin layer of clay. The leather was pitted all over, but in no place pierced through. These ants sometimes get into the joists, floor, or casings of a house and will have them all eaten away but the thinnest shell before they are discovered. You may go to your library and take up what appears to be a perfectly good book and have it crush in your fingers. The ants have devoured the inside. Sometimes they find their way into a trunk and feed on the contents.

Frame houses are built on pillars capped with sheet metal. These are examined periodically to see whether the ants are building their little clay runways over the iron to get into the house. If they are found, they are scraped off and the place tarred. That will keep them away for a time. In the foundation of brick houses, somewhere above the ground is put a layer of hard cement and a sheet of tar paper. The ants cannot go through this and if they come out on the surface of the wall their little telltale runways are seen and taken care of. The drier a house is, the less the danger of white ants.

There is another kind of ant called *"bonkomkom"* (plural, *"benkomkom"*). They feed on a certain kind of tree which bears the same name. At times they migrate like soldiers from one tree to another. They look like large black wasps without wings and sting as severely as hornets. During the early days, at one of the outposts of Mondombe mission station, a man who had five wives beat one of them because she went to church. She ran away to the mission. We had no refuge home, so when her husband came after her and promised that he would let her go to church, I sent her back with him. He was so angry, however, that as soon as they arrived at home he beat her again. She came to the mission a second time and he followed a day or two later. Again I sent her back after he assured me that he would treat her right. He did not whip her this time, but instead tied her to a tree covered with these wasp-like ants. She was stung nearly to death but broke loose and returned to the mission. This time I reported the affair to the nearest government official, who gave her permission to remain permanently at the mission.

Another kind of ant, when bothered, fills the air with an offensive odor. The variety of things African ants can do to make human life miserable is almost unbelievable. Perhaps, however, if we knew of all their work as scavengers and as destroyers of other insects and their larvae, we would feel thankful for the ants.

Hornets are in Congo, and we know it. My wife and I once started off on an itinerary among the villages of the High Tshuapa River country. The first stage of our journey was made by canoe. When we landed to take up the trail, the paddlers ran the canoe aground in the mouth of a shallow creek. The larger part of the canoe extended out in the deep water of the river. In a tree just a few yards in front of the canoe hung a large hornets' nest. As soon as it was discovered, the men in the front end of the canoe fled into the thick brush, while those in the rear jumped into the river and swam off down stream. Three natives stayed with us in the stranded canoe. It was no wonder, after all the confusion, that the hornets were upon us in full force. We fought like mad. A native evangelist stood over Mrs. Moon, fighting them off of her as best he could, while a young fellow wearing only a loin cloth was doing all he could for me. Finally our cook boy jumped into the river and succeeded in getting the canoe off, so that we drifted away with the current. We were fearfully stung all over our faces, necks, and hands, and the boy who was helping me looked as if he had been shot all over with bird-shot. We made our way to the nearest village and rested the rest of that day.

PART TWO

CONGO VILLAGE LIFE

THE CONGO VILLAGE

THE DISTRICT of the Equator in the Belgian Congo is covered with the densest kind of forest. Giant trees are woven together with vines and a thick growth of underbrush that make a jungle almost impenetrable. The only open spots are those that have been cleared by the hand of man, and these if left untended go back to jungle in an incredibly short time. Every station site or garden plot is surrounded by a perpendicular wall of green. As one sails up the narrow streams all that can be seen are these endless green walls rising high on either side. Until recent years even the riverine villages were so completely concealed in the forest that no evidence of their existence was visible from the river. With the ceasing of inter-tribal warfare and the increase of trade along the waterways, the people have cleared away the forest and many villages have good beaches where they keep wood and native foods to sell to the steamers that now ply these waters.

The really typical villages in the Congo are no longer found near the rivers but back in the interior, reached only by jungle trail, a narrow, tortuous footpath through the dense forest. One never goes far in this district without finding swamps. In fact, the swamp is one of the native's units of measure. Although swamps may vary from a few rods to several miles in width, yet if one inquires the distance to the next village, he will be informed that it is just so many swamps away. Of course the strips of land that lie between have no more uniformity of dimension than the swamps. So with this definitely indefinite information as to how far it is, one journeys on, hoping that the swamps are narrow and the crossings good.

We had spent the night in a forest village and were up getting ready for an early start on the jungle path. I asked how far it was to Injolo, our destination for that day. The chief assured me it was just one swamp. At seven o'clock in the morning we waded into the near side of that swamp and at four in the afternoon reached dry land on the other. The chief was perfectly right. It was just one swamp, but what a swamp!

Sometimes, to get a more exact idea of the distance, I would ask, "If I stand up just as the sun rises where will it be when I get to ———— village?" "To stand up" is the colloquial expression meaning "to begin a journey." (There is no use to stand up unless one is going some place!) When they indicated where the sun should be when I arrived, I knew about how far I had to travel.

Some swamps have well-built paths and bridges, while

others must be crossed by wading through mud and water or walking along a string of trees that have been felled at various angles across the swamp and connected by poles laid from one to another. As you walk these trees and poles you are sometimes ten feet up in the air, and again you are feeling with your toes for the log that is submerged under a foot or more of water. Often there is a deep channel of flowing water in the center of the swamp that, in the absence of a bridge, must be crossed in a small dugout canoe. If the party is large, it will necessitate a good many trips and consequently considerable loss of time. Having crossed the swamp, you journey on and at length begin to see daylight through the trees ahead and know that you are nearing the village clearing.

If it is a friendly village—and nearly all are friendly to the missionaries—and if they know ahead that you are coming—and they most likely will, for the coming of any white man is announced ahead over their "radio" drums—the chief and a group of villagers will meet you far out on the path and escort you into the village with singing and dancing.

If the chief is of ordinary rank, you will greet him by saying "*Losako*," which means "proverb" or "motto." Then he replies by giving some short statement of African wisdom such as "*Tocika mbuni* (we leave our marks in the forest)." In other words, "We blaze our trail." If he is a chief of high rank, it is appropriate to greet him with "*Wandao*." He may answer with a proverb or some such word as "*Bikae* (live)" or "*Swa* (blessing)."

If the chief is an *Nkum,* one of the highest rank, which rank is probably more priestly than political, he will be known by the high, stovepipe-like hat which he always wears in public. The brim of this hat is at the top and on top of the hat is tied a beaten brass plate about the size and shape of an ordinary soup plate. When you see one wearing such a hat approaching, you do not speak, but solemnly clap your hands two or three times, according to the rank he holds within the order. He will respond in the same manner as any chief of high rank. Chiefs will often return the courtesy, especially if the visitor is an elderly man, by asking him for his proverb or motto. After the formality of the greeting is over, you may talk freely with any of these chiefs.

The typical village of the forest region consists of one street about as wide as the average American city street, with a row of low thatch-roof houses on each side. Just back of the houses are the banana gardens and beyond the gardens the jungle wall that encloses all.

In this region the houses are rectangular, and where they have not been influenced by the outside world, are seldom over four feet high at the eaves. The roofs are thatched with leaves and the walls are made of leaves between layers of bamboo splints securely tied together. Some of the work is very artistically done. It is customary to have an open veranda-like space in the center of the house, with only a half wall or no wall in front. This is the living room where they cook and eat and lounge about when it is too hot or rainy to sit outside. At each end of the house is a sleeping room entirely enclosed and fitted with a door that can be securely fastened at night. Sometimes the sleeping rooms are small houses completely detached from the living room. In large harems there is one large living room which often has the floor built up of clay a foot or eighteen inches above the level of the ground. Then there is a separate sleeping house for each wife and her children. The style of architecture is rapidly changing in the Congo. The houses are today much higher, and mud is replacing the leaf and bamboo splint for walls.

The Congolese have little in the way of furniture. Their beds are well made of bamboo splints and stand five or six inches high. They are so short that the occupant must either double up or let his legs extend over, which he does according to whether the weather is cold or hot. When a native lies down for a *siesta* in the heat of the day, he says, "I am going to straighten out my legs." When he goes to bed at night he says, "I am going to double up." The Congo people weave beautiful sleeping mats which are spread on the bed or on the ground as they desire.

The tribes living along the lower stretches of the Tshuapa River have much poorer houses and their beds consist of round poles from four to six inches in diameter, split in halves, placed on the ground flat side downward. They sleep on the round sides of those poles without matting or any covering.

Almost everywhere in the district you will find stools of various patterns hewn out of solid blocks of wood. Occasionally a chief will have an elaborate stool about twelve inches high, with four legs and a long curved back. The stool will be about three feet long. These are rare and are handed down from one generation to another in the chief's family. It is seldom that a chief will sell such a chair, for it is the symbol of the authority of the ruling family, and the spirits of ancestors who have sat on it might be displeased.

The first time I tried to buy a stool from the Bolenge chief, he seemed horror-stricken and flatly refused me, as he had a dozen other white men before me who had tried to purchase it. One day to my great surprise he came up to my house bringing the stool with him. He did not wish to sell it, but said he needed some money and wanted to pawn it. I was surprised that he was willing to do even that. I loaned him the money he wanted. Month after month passed by and he did not redeem the stool. As the time for our furlough drew near, I sent for him and said, "If you do not redeem the stool, I will take it with me to America." "No, I can't let you take it," he declared. But just before I was ready to start he came up and said that if I would give him as much more as I had loaned him he would let me keep the stool. I paid him his price. I did not, however, take the stool home with me then, but kept it in Africa another whole term. The chief never went back on his bargain, and I now have the stool with me in America. It is likely that after I had kept it for so many months and nothing had happened to him, he grew bold enough to risk a complete sale.

In the culinary department of the native house one will always find a pestle and mortar, both made of wood. Some foods are beaten on the flat side of the mortar and others in the cavity. There will also be a rough board, resembling a washboard, on which the manioc leaves, which are everywhere used for greens, are rubbed before they are cooked with palm oil and chili peppers.

Food is cooked over open fires in clay pots ten inches to fifteen inches in diameter. Sometimes another clay vessel the same size and shape, but full of holes in the bottom, is placed on top of the pot. Then meat is put in the pot and sweet potatoes, plantain, or sweet manioc roots are placed in the top vessel. Banana leaves are tied over the whole, so that the vegetables are steamed and flavored as the meat cooks. Calabashes are used for carrying water.

While the people depend principally on a vegetable diet, the variety used by any one tribe is very limited. Some tribes depend almost entirely on manioc, from the roots of which a very heavy bread is made. They sometimes use it for fish-bait—no other sinker is needed on the line! Other tribes eat little but plantains, large coarse bananas which are usually cooked before eating. In still other tribes maize is the principal article of diet. A larger variety of food is gradually being used, and the culture and use of rice is spreading.

While the people of Congo limit themselves to very few vegetables, in their animal diet they are almost omniverous. There is hardly anything, from insects to elephants, that they will not eat—crocodiles, monkeys, almost every kind of snake and reptile, dogs, and leopards. Of course there are many animals in the jungle which are fine for eating. I have never tasted anything better than a half-grown wild pig of the Congo. It is richer than our beef and not so greasy as our pork. Then there are eight or ten kinds of antelope, all good eating, ranging from the size of a jack-rabbit to that of an elk. There are buffalo and also the hippopotamus, the meat of which is very much like beef. Some folks think elephants are good eating. We tried some once, but felt about it like the man did about crow pie. He said he "could eat it, but didn't hanker after it."

There is a species of white ant that is eaten which looks much like puffed rice when dried over the fire. Then there is the big fat palm-grub, a dainty morsel. One tribe I know eats roaches. They crumple up loosely a bundle of the leaves used for greens, lay it up in the house, and by morning many of the larger tropical roaches, one and a half to two inches long, are hiding in it. They then pound up the whole mass in the mortar and cook it.

One article of food that I found most universally liked is the caterpillar. Big ones and little ones, woolly ones and smooth ones, black and white, spotted and striped, they are all edible. One day I asked some of the boys to name over the different kinds of caterpillars they ate, and they gave me the names of thirty-four varieties. They ended by saying, "There are some other kinds we eat, but we can't think of the names of them now."

School is an interesting place in caterpillar season. Some of the larger boys will gather a bunch of them on the way to school. They string them like fish and carry the writhing mass into school and hang it up. Many a little fellow will come with one large woolly worm to play with. He "parks" it on the bench beside him while he does his lessons, but it won't stay put. When he gets tired chasing after it, he puts it on his shirtless body. It still travels about, but he knows where it is.

Cannibalism is almost a thing of the past in the Congo, notwithstanding the glaring headlines in the newspapers and the thrilling magazine articles written by Congo travelers while they are safely and comfortably entertained in the home of some missionary or government official. The Belgian Colonial Government has been quite successful in its efforts to stamp out the practice. Some years ago there was a great deal of cannibalism in various sections of the Congo, but even before we left it was only sporadic, occurring during some uprising or at such times as the death of a chief. It is possible that there is occasionally a case that is never brought to light, but this could not often happen with the strict vigilance of the government.

In 1916, Dr. Ernest Pearson and I were traveling in the Ubangi District of the Congo. One day we came into a village as they were having a war dance. The drums were beating and the warriors were dressed and painted in characteristic Congo war style. They were armed with spears, bows and arrows, and old muzzle-loading guns. We asked the chief what the matter was. He pointed to a village about three-quarters of a mile away. "Do you see that village? Sometime ago we fought against it and captured one of their people." (I learned later, from the other village, that this person had been eaten by the victors.) The chief continued: "They then fought against us and captured two and they ate them over there. They are one ahead and we are going back to get even with them." We tried to get the two villages together to settle the affair, but could not. All we could get out of them was: "We'll not fight while you are here, but as soon as you are gone we are going to fight this out."

We had to pass on and we did not learn who had the next feast. But the more I think of it, the more it seems to me that modern warfare is just primitive warfare grown larger. The root causes are the same, mainly fear that someone is going to get ahead of us. It may be some choice oil field, a good naval base, one more battleship—and to keep the other nation from it, we are willing to murder in a more diabolical way than cannibals ever dreamed of.

There is no one individual or tribe that will eat every kind of meat. There are many food taboos, both tribal and individual. Some of the tribal taboos appear to

67

be the relics of an earlier totemism. Individuals may have taboos placed on them by the witch-doctor when they are sick, as a condition of recovery. It may be a temporary taboo or may be for life. There are also sex-taboos, things that members of one sex may not eat, but the others may. The people believe that the spirit or some characteristic of the thing being eaten enters into the eater. The pregnant woman will never eat a hippo, lest her child might look like one. Only the old men, the warriors, may eat a leopard; it makes them fierce and daring. Women must never eat leopard. No man would want the spirit of a leopard to come into his wife.

If the natives are around the village they eat a little breakfast about nine o'clock in the morning. Those who go off hunting or fishing start early, taking with them only a little piece of native bread or a stalk of sugar cane. The women who go to work all day in their gardens take with them little or nothing to eat. In the evening the women return with their baskets well filled with produce from the garden and with a large bundle of wood tied on top. The men are back from hunting or fishing, and while they are living over again every detail of the day's experiences, the women are busy getting the one big meal of the day, which is eaten just after dark. Then the night is before them for story or play.

As one starts through a village, the first place of interest he sees is the dance hall. This is not a large pavilion, but just the open street which is kept beautifully clean. With their little brooms about eighteen inches long the women keep their houses, the front and back yards, and the streets well swept. There is no dirt or filth lying around a real native village. The dirty village is one composed of detribalized natives who have lost all the virtues of their own life and have acquired only the least desirable traits of the Europeans.

In the smooth village path the folk gather to dance. Here during the light of the moon they dance, dance, dance, all night long and sometimes all the next day. No one who has seen them dance would ever again accuse the African of being lazy. They seem never to get tired. All the emotions of life are danced. Victory and defeat, joy and sorrow, love and hate are expressed by the Congo people through the rhythm of motion.

Occasionally you will see a group of men or women or a mixed group that has practiced some special dances and tumbling acts, performing during the day; then at night there is a free-for-all dance. The special actors are paid by free-will contributions thrown out to them during the performance.

The next place of interest to visit is the "city hall." This is sometimes a thatched shelter, but more frequently it is just a large tree left standing in the center of the village. Some crude seats are placed in the shade of the tree, and here the chief meets with the elders of the village to talk over all the affairs of village life. This is an open forum where absolute freedom of speech is maintained. Here is the court where men settle their differences. Here are tried all criminals and breakers of tribal laws. The accused and the witnesses for or against (who are voluntary, not summoned) may speak as often and as long as they choose. The African is never more at home than when he is "talking a palaver." There one often hears charming outbursts of eloquence and pleasing bits of native wit and humor. There is an African proverb which says, "The Lord taught the white man how to write, but the black man how to speak." There seems to be at least some truth in the comparison.

When there is nothing else on hand they sometimes turn the forum into a debating society. The debaters for each side are not chosen beforehand, but each one defends *with many words* the side he chooses. No vote is taken at the end, so nothing is ever settled. One question I have heard debated a number of times is: "Which was created first, the animal or vegetable kingdom?"

Another very important center of village life is the blacksmith shop. The metal-working art was highly developed among the Bantu before the modern white man ever entered Central Africa. They mined iron, smelted it over charcoal fires, and made their knives, hoes, axes, and the metal points for spears and arrows. They also mined copper and this became the principal metal for their jewelry. The traders soon recognized the value of such metals for barter and began to ship in large quantities of iron bars and brass wire. It was much easier for the natives to gather wild rubber, gum copal, palm nuts, and other products of the country and exchange them for the imported metals, than it was to work their own mines. As a consequence, the native mines have fallen into disuse.

The smith is a very important man in the village. He not only makes all the tools and weapons, but also manufactures the jewelry and makes the money for the tribe. You will see in his shop brass or copper anklets weighing from a few ounces to ten or twelve pounds each, smaller rings for the wrists and arms, and neck rings weighing up to twenty or twenty-five pounds. The anklets and neck rings, when put on, are driven together in such a way that it requires another operation of the blacksmith to remove them, which is dangerous and sometimes very painful.

Occasionally you will see men wearing rings on necks, wrists, or ankles, but the extremely heavy jewelry is reserved for the favorite wives. The favorite wife of a wealthy polygamist may be decked with a supply of jewelry that weighs upwards of thirty pounds. While wearing these heavy articles of jewelry, the women are not permitted to travel on the river in the canoes, for if the canoe should sink the jewelry would be lost. Of course the husband would also hate to see the woman lost, for she is part of his riches. A man's wealth and social standing are largely reckoned by the number of wives he has.

When an important visitor, such as a chief from some neighboring tribe or a white man, comes to town, the village chief or someone operating for him will broadcast over the drum the announcement of his arrival and ask the women of the village to bring food for the visitor's caravan. When the guest leaves, his departure is sounded forth so that the next village may know about when to expect him. As he marches off, a farewell greeting and a few words of caution may echo down the forest trail from the deep, mellow tones of the village drum: "Farewell, old man. Choose your path wisely. Be careful; the paths are slippery today."

The tribes of the Central Congo Basin living in the great forest along the Equator were until recently the least influenced by cultural diffusion from without of any Congo tribes. Their ancestors, having received (from no one knows where) the wonderful Bantu forms of speech and the metal-working art, have handed them on to their forest children. But from historic times until recent years cultural contact with the outside world was very limited. Even the Arab slave raids that reached almost every part of Africa did not penetrate here. Along the headwaters of the Tshuapa River will be found the extreme limit to which they penetrated before being turned back. In that section, many natives will still be found who bear the Arab slave mark, a hole through the ear for a man slave or through one side of the nostril for a woman slave. The natives told me that the Arabs' method was to take a large needle threaded with raffia and pierce the ear or nose, drawing the raffia through the hole and leaving it there. If the ear or nostril bled, that person was taken out and killed as being possessed of an evil spirit.

Most of the District of the Equator remained in ignorance of the outside world until the coming of the rubber agents, who exacted such heavy toll of the native people in labor and in life. During the days of the rubber atrocities, which came to an end just before we reached the Congo, tens of thousands of natives lost their lives or were left crippled for life. The rubber agents, if not satisfied with the amount of rubber brought in by a village, would seize natives and cut off hands, feet, lips, or ears to punish them. Sometimes small children were thus mutilated to punish the parents. For years the natives were haunted by a fear that the rubber days might return. Many times while out hunting I have seen the hunters stop to dig up and destroy rubber vines, lest they should again be compelled to bring in wild rubber. Even during World War II, when they were asked to bring in wild rubber they refused until assured by the missionaries that it was not a trick to bring back the old rubber days.

The Congo Village

I have described some, but by no means all, of the Congo I saw from the village street. At first one only sees thatched houses, banana gardens, clay pots, spears, bows and arrows, and naked savages; but the longer one lives among the Congo people the more evident it is that to understand them one must see much that is beyond these simple material things of their culture. This will be more clearly seen in the succeeding chapters.

CHAPTER II

MARRIAGE CUSTOMS AND NAMES

THE MEDIUM-SIZED anklet weighing from three to five pounds is the real money of the forest native, and often nothing else will be accepted in payment of the marriage price. The marriage price leads us to one of the most complex phases of Bantu culture. There is by no means uniformity of practice in regard to the marriage price among Bantu tribes. But one thing is certain—it is nowhere regarded by them as merely buying and selling women. The payment of the marriage price is the real marriage ceremony.

This may be illustrated from the practice of the tribes on the High Tshuapa. The first wife of the son is often arranged for while the boy is quite young, his father giving an occasional present to the father of the prospective bride. The children do not begin life as husband and wife until about the age of puberty. We have had boys in our schools under ten years of age who could tell us who their "wives" were.

If a young man is old enough to take part in the choosing of his wife he may indicate as the object of his affection a girl in some other clan—never a member of his own, for they are exogamous. When he has named the girl of his preference, his father and the elders of his clan will go to talk it over with the girl's father and the elders of her clan. If it is agreeable all around, a few anklets are given to the father of the girl and she goes to live with her husband. The marriage price is always paid on the instalment plan, never all at once. If the husband is too slow about making subsequent payments, the father of the girl coaxes her home and keeps her until a suitable amount is forthcoming, when she returns to her husband. In case of a disagreement between the husband and the wife's people, the wife always sides with her people against her husband.

Before the birth of the first child the expectant mother returns to her people. The child is born in the home of its maternal grandparents, where mother and babe remain until the husband comes with a handsome present to reclaim them.

There are many other things involved in the payment of the marriage price. We are speaking of the marriage of freeborn equals. A man might buy for a cash price a slave woman, who becomes in a sense a wife. This woman he owns and treats about as he pleases. He cannot do that with a freeborn woman whom he marries by paying the marriage price in the regular way. When the husband gives and the father receives the anklets, the payment stands as a guarantee of fair play

76

on both sides. The father and his clan have guaranteed to furnish the husband with a wife who will fulfill all the wifely duties according to their standards. This always includes the bearing of children, and should she fail, he may return his wife and get his money back or another wife in her place. If his wife runs away without any provocation the husband does not follow her, but goes to her father and demands the return of his money. The father cannot comply, for as soon as he acquired this new source of income by the marriage of his daughter, he added a new wife to his own harem and must pass the money on to her father as fast as he gets it. So instead of attempting to return the money, he compels the daughter to return to her husband.

If the husband mistreats his wife beyond the standards allowed for husbandly discipline, and the wife runs off, she may stay away and the husband has no recourse. By his mistreatment he has broken the contract.

Another interesting phase of the marriage price is revealed in case of serious illness on the part of the wife. If the husband fears she is going to die, he will send her back to her own people. For if she dies there the father will have to refund the price received, but if she dies in the house of her husband he will be held responsible for her death and can make no reclaim.

In the early days of the mission at Bolenge, a man in the native village took a wife from a village a few miles away. She was afterward taken sick with sleeping sickness, and when she became seriously ill her husband sent her to her father. The father returned her to her husband, and again the husband sent her back to the father. For days they kept the poor woman on the trail between the villages, each trying to escape the responsibility of her death. One day she sat down by the jungle trail, fell asleep, and never wakened. After her death neither husband nor father would go near her, for the one so doing would be held responsible. She became, in the words of one of the native proverbs, "a corpse of the woods." This expresses the ultimate in being friendless—there is no one even to bury you when you are dead. When the word came to the mission, the Christians of the village made a coffin and gave the woman a decent burial.

There is, of course, no end of palavers in trying to settle these husband-and-wife affairs. Many personal fights and clan and tribal wars have been fought over Congo women. There is no other one thing that takes so much of the native's time and nothing presents so many complex and baffling problems.

Different missions have used various methods in handling the native marriage question, but almost any missionary will say that he thinks his mission might have done better if it had adopted some different policy. To the early missionaries of the Disciples of Christ Congo Mission the native marriage looked like a pure case of buying and selling women, and one must admit that there is much to justify that view. Young men who have been disinherited because they become Christians, and have no clan to help them pay a large price, find it difficult to get wives. Sometimes even mercenary Christian parents have refused to let their daughter marry some Christian boy whom she loved, preferring to marry her to some wealthy polygamist who was able to give a handsome marriage price. Seeing these and many other attendant evils, the mission took a strong stand against the marriage price, refusing to let Christians receive any at all.

This decision was of little import to the non-Christian natives, for they did not want to marry their daughters to Christians; but the Christian men were dependent on the non-Christians for wives. Because so many women were in polygamous homes and were completely under the control of their husbands, one would find many more men than women in the church in the early days of mission work in the Congo.

A real situation is created when a Christian young man upon the death of his father falls heir to a large harem. From the day of his father's death the women are considered his wives and they call him husband. He at once becomes a great man in the tribe, with the wealth and prestige of his father. There may be in the inherited harem some young women his own age that are especially appealing to him. If he wishes to give any of the wives or his own sisters or his mother in marriage, the marriage price comes to him. Not only is there this temptation of wealth and standing, but in the eyes of the whole tribe, these women and their children are his family, and if he refuses to look after them, he is a slacker and a disgrace to the name of his father. He is breaking every tradition of his tribe concerning the duty of a son at such a time. It was especially hard for one in the earlier days to make proper disposal of inherited women, since the mission had ruled that no Christian should receive any marriage price for them. Even under this rigorous ruling many young men were true to the church.

I believe that with a better understanding and a sympathetic appreciation of the situation the missionaries might often have been of greater help in such cases. There is no doubt a chance for much evil in connection with the receiving of money in exchange for wives, but I doubt whether chances for abuse are any greater than the evils that have arisen out of considering the marriage price a mere matter of barter in women.

How deeply this whole system is grounded in the thinking of the native people is seen from the following circumstance. The mission was determined to strike out this apparently evil custom not only by legislation but by demonstration. The opportunity came when some orphan girls left in charge of the mission came to the marriageable age. Some young men very closely connected with the mission began to notice their charms and got up courage enough to ask the missionaries if they might marry them. This was the missionaries' opportunity to show them what a real Christian marriage should be, without the taint of money. The couples were given careful instructions in the meaning of married life and were united in the church, by a beautiful wedding ceremony that had been translated, with some adaptations, from the English. Several couples at various times were married in this same manner and all seemed well for a time.

Then trouble began. When some misunderstanding arose to interrupt their marriage bliss, the wife would accuse the husband of being so poor, and without any family of standing to help him, that he had to go to the mission where he could get a wife for nothing. He would retort that she was so worthless that they were glad to give her away to get rid of her. According to their own customs, they were not married. Neither the reputation nor the wealth of family or clan was involved on either side. Such failures were so frequent that the mission finally assumed the position of the girl's family and asked a nominal marriage price. Such marriages proved more satisfactory than those where no payment was involved. The rule against the receiving of the marriage price by a Christian has gone very largely into the discard.

Among the Congo people it was customary for every man to marry as many wives as possible. Some chiefs have counted their women by scores or even hundreds. This led to much evil, for it left many men without wives. But grand polygamy is breaking up under the pressure of missions and of commerce. Under the old regime every woman was an economic asset. She made the clothing for herself and her children, the mats on which they all slept, the pots she cooked in, the red powder and palm oil they used on their bodies and hair, and raised all the food the family ate, with a surplus to sell in the public market.

The monogamic families of the native Christians set a new standard. The women began to wear dresses in place of the raffia fringe or banana leaf. Some cooked in enameled pots instead of the black clay pots of their own manufacture. The highly scented cosmetics and pomades sold by the trader began to replace the old red powder and palm oil. There are many happy Christian homes in which the new woman has found her true place and is a real asset; but when the women in a large harem begin to imitate their monogamic sisters they are a decided liability to their husband. When thirty or forty wives go to their husband and say that they are not going to work for him any more unless he buys each one a dress, and then refuse to cook until he buys each an enameled kettle, he sees bankruptcy staring him in the face, and his plight becomes worse as the demand for l u x u r i e s grows. The government then adds the last straw by imposing a head tax on all of a man's wives but one. One is a necessity, but others are luxuries. Thus by the new standard of living set by the monogamous family, together with the economic pressure, women in harems are now luxuries that but a few men can afford in large numbers.

One day the chief of Bolenge came up to the mission and said: "White Man, what am I going to do? I have twenty-three wives and I am starving to death. Not one of them will cook anything for me to eat." His wives had gone on a sit-down strike, demanding that he buy each one a dress like the Christian women were wearing. When he finally got his strike settled, they called another, demanding that he furnish them with enameled cooking ware to replace their old clay pots. No wonder the chief had to part with valuable heirlooms he had received from his ancestors!

The colonial government is making an effort to discourage grand polygamy; but any social custom that is as deeply imbedded in the life of the people as polygamy is in Africa, dies hard. The system lends itself to abuse by clever rascals. State-appointed chiefs use their power and authority to increase their own wealth. Some of these invest their riches in women. By buying girls when they are still small, a chief can get a corner on the wife market of his tribe. He soon has a large harem and demands exorbitant prices if anyone wishes to purchase a wife from him. When a strict, understanding, law-enforcing Belgian official is appointed to his particular area, the chief "farms" out his wives so it appears that he has but one. He thus increases his own income. When such an official is replaced by one who is lax and winks at native practices, the chief again gathers his harem about him. Polygamy is still Congo's number one headache for both the missionary and the sincere government official.

Human names and how they are given is always a matter of great interest among primitive peoples. I was called "Ikoko," until our first child was born, a boy. The natives named him "Iluku" after one of the greatest chiefs of that section. Then they followed their own custom and called me "Is' Iluku," and Mrs. Moon "Nyango Iluku." We were the father and mother of Iluku. It would be a disgrace, until they were old, to call parents by any other name than that of the father and mother of their firstborn child. The natives called me Is' Iluku until the last term I was in the Congo. I was then becoming more bald and gray and more proficient in their language, more ready in answering with their proverbs, and able more generally to enter into their life and folkways. So they judged me old enough to be initiated into their degree of "Old Man," the honorary degree of the Congo.

A large group of natives came up one evening and different ones stood up and gave me a lecture on how an old man should act. Among other things they said, "He should be generous; he should never be hasty in his judgments." In fact, they gave me much advice that would be good for any old man to follow. Then they said, "From now on you will be known as 'Ejim' Ikoko (the old man Ikoko).'" According to their custom, they went back to my first Congo name, "Ikoko," and prefixed their word for old man, "Ejimo."

They have not called Mrs. Moon "the old woman" yet, but if they should it would be just as much of an honor, for the one thing they reverence and respect in their social organization is old age. If either men or women in Congo ever misrepresent their age, it is to make themselves appear much older than they really are, because of the respect every one has for the aged.

It was in Congo that I received a doctor of science degree. Because of the much building I did during my missionary service, the natives called me "the doctor of the wisdom of building houses (*nkanga ea wanya wa ntungy' ilombe*)."

Among the Congolese, as among most primitive people, some circumstance at the time of birth may suggest the name of the child. It is a disgrace in Congo for a married woman to be childless. In one village a woman who had no children was laughed at by the successful mothers. When after many years she gave birth to a boy baby she named him "Stop-your-laughing."

The mission used to make all of its lumber by hand, with pit-saws. A sawyer was working on a tree they called *bolekwa* when his wife gave birth to a girl baby. They named her "Bolekwa."

When a Congo man marries he wants to become the father of many children, both boys and girls. If the first one is not a boy, he is very much disappointed. A young man married the daughter of a chief and of course had to pay a handsome marriage price, fifty thousand brass rods. Their first child was a girl. When they showed the baby to the father, in his disappointment he said, "My fifty thousand rods that are destroyed!" They named the child that, shortening the name for practical purposes to "Bakesi (tens of thousands)." That sounded very aristocratic, for a girl worth tens of thousands of rods was considered of real class!

Sometimes a child is called by some fictitious name

rather than by its real name, in an attempt to deceive the evil spirits they believe are ever lurking about to carry off little children. If some family has lost several children in infancy, the next child may be called "Filth" or some unmentionable name. They reason that, when the spirits hear them calling a child by such a name, they will decide that a child who is worth no better name than that is not worth taking, and will pass it by.

Chapter III

LANGUAGE AND COMMUNICATION

WHEN we first stepped ashore on the banks of the Congo at the Equator we did not know a word of any African tongue. We could not even say "How do you do?" or "Good-bye." However, we soon began to try to express ourselves, and like all beginners in a foreign country speaking a strange language, we at first fell into many amusing mistakes.

When we had been there some months, one day a widow came up from the village and asked Mrs. Moon for some palm nuts, widely used for food by both the native people and foreigners. They grow in large clusters very densely knit together. There was a bunch under the kitchen table at the time and, pointing to the nuts, Mrs. Moon attempted to say: "There is a bunch. Get down there and shell off the nuts." But instead she said: "There is the bunch. Get down there and blow your nose."

The woman understood what she meant and began to shell off the nuts; but when Mrs. Moon looked around, the boy she was training for a cook had slipped in behind the kitchen door and was trying to suppress his laughter. Mrs. Moon asked, "Now, what mistake have I made that is causing you to laugh like that?" He replied, "No, no, *Mama,* that was right!" "No," she persisted, "I have made some mistake and you are laughing at it. Tell me what it was so I will not make it again." Still he insisted that what she said was right. Then Mrs. Moon became firm. "Look here, we have come to teach you people, but we can't do it unless we know your language, and you must be my language teacher, for you work in the house with me. If I go around making mistakes, everybody will laugh at you and say that you do not know how to teach *Mama* the language." He then said, "Well, *Mama,* you told that woman to blow her nose." The word for "palm nuts" is *mba,* and the verb "to blow the nose" is *emba.*

The first work the mission gave me to do in the Congo was to take charge of a group of young men in the carpenter shop. After working with them for a few days, I wrote to my family in America: "I am working signs and wonders out here. I make signs and these people wonder what I mean."

The sign language of the African is quite different from ours. If you should beckon anyone as we do here, he would wonder what you meant. They beckon with the p a l m downward by repeatedly drawing in the fingers. If you should point at anything with the finger, everybody would look at your finger to see what is the matter with it. They point with their lips.

With the exception of the Hottentot-Bushman group of South Africa, all the languages spoken by the natives from the southern tip of the continent to the Equator, and somewhat beyond in Central and West Africa, belong to the Bantu language family. In *A Comparative Study of Bantu and Semi-Bantu Languages*,[1] Sir Harry Johnston gives samples of two hundred twenty-six Bantu languages. These languages often vary so much that natives of different tribes cannot understand each other, yet there is a basic similarity in grammar and vocabulary that distinctly shows a common origin.

Jean Kenyon Mackenzie, in an article in the *Atlantic Monthly* of November, 1916, says: "The Bantu is betrayed entirely by his speech. He has no history except as traced and exhibited in his speech; he has no physical distinction or type—only a typical language, and no cohesion except the cohesion of language."[2] The Bantu languages are not simple jargons of a few hundred words in which one can express the mere necessities of life, but are real languages, highly organized, with large and rich vocabularies.

As to the value and future of Bantu languages, there are differences of opinion. Dr. C. T. Loram says: "The Native tongues must give place to the more practical European languages. Apart from sentiment there is no reason for wishing the Bantu languages to survive. They have served their purpose. They are not capable of expressing the ideas which the new European civilization has brought to the country. They are hopelessly clumsy and inadequate on the mathematical and scientific side."[3]

The other extreme is taken by Dr. Diedrich Wester-

---

[1] Oxford University Press, publishers.

[2] From "The Bulu and His Women." Used by permission.

[3] From *The Education of the South African Native,* by C. T. Loram. Used by permission of the publishers, Longmans, Green & Co., Inc.

mann, who says: ". . . the Gospel and the whole of Christian education must take root in the mother soil of the vernacular. Only in this way will it enter into the African mind and become the medium of a new life. . . A people without a language and a tradition of its own is individually dead, it has become part of the mass instead of being a living personality." He expresses his belief that "not only the Africans, but the African languages, have a future, and (that) at least some of these will one day rank among the literary languages of the world."[1]

It may be true that the Bantu languages are "clumsy" and "inadequate" for mathematical and scientific purposes, but their natural flexibility and the readiness with which new words are borrowed or formed give great hope for the future. To give a Bantu a word is to give him a group of words, for he applies his own system of forming derivatives. To illustrate from the Lokundo, the Bantu language of the District of the Equator in the Belgian Congo, we may use the word *mesa* (table), introduced by the Portuguese. The natives, observing the custom of white men in the tropics sitting around the table visiting, soon began to use *mesa* as a verb, meaning "to visit." Then it was only natural to derive *bomesi* (a visitor), *jimeso* (a visit), *emeselo* (a visiting or a visiting place).

Whatever is the ultimate future of Bantu, it should be used now for at least four reasons. First, there is the need to preserve the unwritten literature of these peoples. There has perhaps never been found another unwritten language as rich in folklore, proverbs, and poetry as the Bantu. The Bantu have built no monument, have left no

---

[1] From "The Place and Function of the Vernacular in African Education," by Dr. Diedrich Westermann, in *International Review of Missions,* January, 1925. Used by permission of International Missionary Council.

records in writing or painting, they have no history, nothing that tells of past achievements or present greatness, except what is built into and transmitted by means of their wonderful language.

Second, the Bantu cannot be understood apart from his language. "Mental life has evolved in each people an individual shape and a proper mode of expression; in this sense we speak of the soul of a people, and the most immediate, the most adequate, exponent of the soul of a people is its language."[1] Inter-tribal wars, systems of slavery and polygamy, agriculture and metal-working, and all other characteristics of the Bantu people, seem to dwarf into insignificance when compared with their language. And the white man will never know what is "back of the black man's mind" until he is assisted in his exploration by a thorough knowledge of the native tongue. The Bantu's best, highest, noblest concepts live in and are transmitted by his language; when he loses his language he loses all.

Third, the native language is the only possible means of reaching the present generation with a system of education. The fact that a number of Congolese have an elementary education and are now able to teach the lower grades in their vernacular makes the beginnings of education possible in thousands of native villages. Today there would probably be schools in no more than a score of villages if teaching had to be done in French only; and if the Congo has to wait for the development of a teaching force capable of teaching in a foreign tongue, there is no hope for the present generation and little for the next.

Fourth, if any foreign language should be forced upon

[1] Dr. Diedrich Westermann, ibid.

so large an uneducated population, it would soon become so corrupt as to be practically useless. Hybrid jargons that grow up under such conditions are almost unintelligible, both to the natives and to the foreigners whose languages have been chopped up together to form a new linguistic "hash."

The Lonkundo, the native language of the Disciples of Christ Congo Mission area, like other Bantu languages, had never been written until the missionaries began to reduce it to writing. They found that it had three regular conjugations of verbs, eleven classes of nouns, and quite an elaborate system of relative, temporal, and conditional clauses. Sentences in Bantu languages are bound together by alliterative concording prefixes, which when spoken give them a mellifluence seldom if ever heard in other languages.

No consideration of the language of Central Africa would be complete if it neglected the highly developed "drum language" used for purposes of communication from village to village. This drum language is quite an enigma to the white man. It is not phonetic, at least in the same sense as is the Morse code. When white men have tried to test the ability of the native to speak with the drum they have usually been disappointed. Very likely that was because they suggested a message that was foreign to native thought and custom.

I believe that the drum language is largely the language of proverbs, where a whole sentence or paragraph is summed up in one word. One might be quite proficient in their everyday language and yet be unable to understand them when they choose to speak in proverbs. Their proverbs have grown out of their own community life, so that anything within the range of their own experiences they can express in proverbs or on the drum. Certain beats on the two-toned drum stand for certain proverbs which are thought units. The Congolese will sometimes telegraph in the same way by imitating the two tones of the drum in whistling, or by use of the two-toned trumpet made from the horn of an antelope or tusk of an elephant.

Drums vary according to their use. Some skin-covered drums are used for dancing, but the *lokoli,* the big drum of all purposes, including communication, is made from a section of a solid hardwood log. It may be two feet in diameter and about six feet in length. A slot an inch and a half or so in width is cut in the top side, running almost the entire length of the section of log. The ends are left solid, and through this one opening the inside is hollowed out. By cleverly shaping the cavity and leaving one lip thicker than the other, the drum is made to give two distinct tones as it is struck alternately on the two lips near the center of the drum. The drummer, standing at the side of the drum and using two large soft-wood drumsticks, skillfully intermingles these two tones.

A large drum is always to be found near the chief's place, and a lesser drum in each section of the village. The larger drums can be heard under favorable conditions twelve to fifteen miles. They are in constant use for communication between villages. Perhaps no primitive people has ever devised a more clever and effective means of sending messages over long distances than the two-toned drum of Equatorial Africa.

The Congo drum is more than a means of communication, however. It is inseparably a part of every phase of native living. Rhythm is the very bloodstream of Congo life and the throbbing of the drum is the heartbeat. The Congo people eat, they sing, they work, they play, they

93

paddle their canoes, to the rhythm of the drum. The drum is used in times of sorrow and rejoicing, in peace and war, night and day.

One day in the village near the mission station a celebration was being held. A large group of men were singing and dancing to the rhythm of the drums. Not less than a dozen drums of various sizes were beating in perfect time. At the largest drum stood the most famous drummer of that district. While he was not breaking the rhythm, he was beating in such a way that he was broadcasting dance calls or whatever else occurred to him of interest. Andrew Hensey, my senior in missionary service, and I went out to look on a while.

As we approached the crowd in company with one of the natives, this man turned to Mr. Hensey and said, "The man at the big drum is asking you for your *losako.*" That is, he was giving Mr. Hensey the greeting of honor. Then the drummer began to sound forth Mr. Hensey's praise on the drum. He told how this white man was just like a father to them and they were all his children. After a bit the native turned to me: "Now he is giving you the greeting of honor." Then the drum sounded a hymn of praise about me, telling how I had built their church and the steamer, and how with my gun I had often satisfied their hunger by killing game for them.

As one travels up the Momboyo River there is a large horseshoe bend just before Lotumbe is reached. At the narrow neck of the land, it is not far across to the station. At this point we used to blow the whistle of the *Oregon,* and it could be clearly heard at the mission. It was then a full hour before we could steam around the large bend to the mission beach. One day when I blew the whistle at that point we heard the Lotumbe drum. The native pilot smiled and said, "They say they heard us before we blew the whistle."

In villages along the High Tshuapa River, after the death of an important individual a near relative will go to the big drum each morning about four o'clock and for some time will broadcast the praise of the departed and their love and devotion to him. This is kept up for some weeks. It is intended to keep the spirit in a good humor so he will not bother the living.

The drum is thus telegraph, radio, telephone, orchestra, religious instrument, all in one. I have even heard men quarrelling by use of drums over a distance of several miles. I always felt that if you had to quarrel, that was a good way to do it.

CHAPTER IV

FOLK-SONGS, PROVERBS, FABLES

O WAJWELA *mbul'a ngonda, ebwela na? Lolango.* (Why are we rained upon in the woods? [Because of] love.)" We were on the jungle path when the rain began to pour, but the carriers were well fed and happy and they started this beautiful chorus. It is only one of hundreds of literary jewels to be found in the large volume of "unwritten literature" of Bantu peoples. One seems to be speaking paradoxically in using the term "unwritten literature," for literature is written; but I know of no better term for that large mass of stories, songs, and proverbs found in some unwritten tongues. It is largely around the campfire and on the trail that the wonderful language of the Congolese has been kept alive and the wealth of their literature preserved.

The folklore of any primitive people is never the product of careful study and planning. It is rather the spontaneous expression of the emotions of life, such as joy, love, hate. If the form of the expression is unusual or striking, it will probably live and be handed on as a part of the unwritten literature. As folklore precedes written literature, it depends entirely upon the memory and is orally transmitted from one generation to the next. It is the product of the community and cannot live unless it is in harmony with the thought and life of the group. Sometimes there is found in it the keenest sense of humor. Folklore is the textbook of the primitive, yet in its earlier stages there is no conscious effort at moralizing or teaching.

One other characteristic of folklore is that it is almost universally expressed in rhythm. The rhythm of words and the rhythm of motion, song and dance, are always present. Any form of work possible in the Congo will be turned into a semi-dance and performed with much unnecessary motion. The greatest asset to any canoe crew, caravan, or work group is a good song-leader. It is almost an axiom in Africa, "No singing, no working." Whether pushing a steamboat off the sand-bank or pulling a dead hippo out of the water, the task is performed with an equal amount of song and rhythmic motion.

One day in the edge of a swamp I saw a native rouge factory. In the Congo, rouge is made by rubbing together blocks of the deep red camwood, with a little sand between, thus grinding them into a powder. The powder is used with palm oil in the hair and on the body by old and young of both sexes. Formerly almost every household had a couple of these blocks where the woman sat and ground during her leisure moments.

Here in the edge of the swamp was a large camwood log beside which stood a dozen women. Each woman had a block of the same wood in her hands. As they sang their songs, with rhythmic motion they rubbed their blocks on the smooth spots on the top of the log and ground out the red powder.

Like Hebrew poetry, the Lonkundo songs have the rhythm of accents rather than an exact number of syllables, and if they rhyme it seems to be purely accidental. One well-metered little verse is the following:

> *Ompampa l'akonga*
> *Omeka nk'akonga*
> *Bakong'ondimola*
> *Benyaku a mpoke.*
> (Nothing and *bakonga* [tiny fish],
> Try the *bakonga,*
> The *bakonga* will take out, for me,
> The green plantain from the pot.)

Benyaku are unsavory half-grown green plantains and are hard to eat unless one has some kind of meat sauce to eat with them. The natives will often go hungry rather than eat the *benyaku* alone. The idea in the verse is that a man goes fishing and returns with only a few tiny fish and his friends laugh at him; but he replies that the *bakonga* are better than nothing, for they will flavor the plantains so he can eat them. Otherwise they would remain untouched in the pot. It is like our proverb, "A little is better than nothing."

Native proverbs are terse statements of truth and wisdom based on a people's own experiences and observations. There are proverbs touching every phase of Bantu life. In them will be found their social and civil codes. It is a case of betrayed friendship, an unfaithful husband or wife, disrespectful children? There is always a proverb to fit. Here is their Blackstone, from which the chief quotes when he gives his decision in difficult cases. Here also is found their standard of business ethics, which in some cases reminds one of the standards held by some in the West, where cunning and craftiness are rewarded above honesty. And here are their unwritten moral and religious codes, and their philosophy.

When spoken, proverbs are usually given in a very abbreviated form, sometimes in only one word, and on first hearing need to be explained. A proverb is often a moral drawn from some elaborate story.

The following are a few of the proverbs I collected while in Congo:

Wanganga, jituka nda nsalo.

The magpie (is) pretty in feathers.

The natives do not consider the magpie good for food and use the proverb to express hypocrisy. Another of the same meaning is:

Iko'tuka besof'ololo.

The porcupine (is) pretty (but) the intestines (are bitter).

The following might be spoken to a man suspected of stealing:

Mba itswa l'onto.

Palm nuts go off with a man.

That is, they do not disappear of their own accord. If missing, someone has taken them.

100

Folk-Songs, Proverbs, Fables

A warning against misplaced confidence:

Ofonga yoko nd'omwa wa nsombo?
Do you put your bread away in the mouth of a hog?

A work of necessity:

Bomoto akimaka nsoso l'osamba wa jwende.
A woman runs after a chicken because of the lack of a man.

If a woman is seen running after a chicken, it is a sure sign she has no husband.

Once while I was captain of our mission steamer, the *Oregon,* I was about ready to start on one of our regular trips, four hundred miles down river to the head of the Congo railway. We always did considerable buying for both missionaries and natives on these trips. One of our station foremen brought me some money and asked me to get him a pair of shoes. I accused him of buying for someone else and not for himself, and he replied with the following proverb:

Ifulu ntakotswaka bonkena la mbimbi ey'oninga.
The bird does not fly from the *bonkena* (a kind of fruit tree) because its friend is satisfied.

He also gave me this one, which has the same meaning:

Nkoi ntakumbaka nyama la jwilo j'oninga.
The leopard does not seize its prey because its friend is hungry.

Another similar proverb is:

Nsombo ntacimela webi bonkufu.

The hog does not dig *bonkufu* (sweet manioc roots) for his friend.

Bribery is expressed by:

Ngelo y'otso.

Brass rods (money) of the night.

If you pay the judge the night before you may get a favorable decision.

A proverb regarding divided affection, indecision, is:

Jumba l'öna
Betem'efe.

The treasure and the child (and) two stomachs.

(The stomach is used as the seat of affection.)

They explain this proverb by the story of a woman who crossed the river with her baby in a very small canoe to work in her garden. While there she found a valuable treasure. The canoe was too small for her to take both treasure and child back to the village at once. If she left the treasure, someone might steal it before she could return for it. If she left the child, the leopard might get it. So there she was, with her divided heart, unable to decide what to do.

To indicate the impossible:

Onjemy'a nkema.

You cause me to stand on a monkey.

Loola ntakitak'oamba.

The sky is not reached with a stick.

Basi nd'omwa, ko fetsa tsa.

Water in the mouth and blow the fire.

Sympathy:

> *Jiso aolela, jolo aoföla.*
>
> (When) the eye cries, the nose runs.

A hidden sorrow:

> *Boninga aolela, mpisaji afeana l'asi.*
>
> The *boninga* (a kind of fish) cries, but its tears are not known because of the water.

Do not laugh at another's misfortune:

> *Otabwe bolo, tosekak'etumbe.*
>
> Who is not dead in strength, should not laugh at the lame.

The suggested idea is that one may sometime lose his strength. It reminds one of Proverbs 27:1—"Boast not thyself of tomorrow, for thou knowest not what a day may bring forth."

Preparedness:

> *Bofala wemi, osingu bokulu.*
>
> The *bofala* (a kind of antelope) is standing, you are making a string.

That is, the animal is standing there, but you cannot shoot for you are just making your bow-string, which you should have done long before the hunting season arrived.

Real rank is known:

> *Ole la mpifo, ntakösulaka.*
>
> Who has rank does not cough.

If an insignificant person is present, he is continually coughing or doing something to attract attention; but if a man of real rank comes, he walks in quietly, without any pretensions whatsoever, but is always recognized and receives the honor due him.

Rebuke for a pestiferous person:
Losizi ntafikak'entuku.
A louse does not respect an elder.

Bad bargains:
Ntasombaka wato wine.
One does not buy a sunken canoe.
That is like buying a "pig in the poke."

Ifak'imönkölö, k'osomba nsoso, mpawosese nyama lae?
One knife, and you buy a chicken (with the knife); how will you cut up the meat?

A cash transaction:
Ambya, ambola.
Put down (the price), pick up (the article).

The two following came from the creation stories:
Nsombo afiman'aseke l'ekuto.
The hog was denied horns because of tardiness.

He came late the day they were giving out horns and they were all gone when he arrived.

Ngubu afiman'atoi l'efösö.
The hippo was denied ears because of noise.

He was making so much noise he did not hear when they called his name. When he finally came all the ears were gone except the tiny little ears he has.

In times of joy, we forget our sorrow:

Wane aolofela mbula.

The sunshine forgets the rain.

The doctor forgets his own medicine:

Nkanga aolofela bokumbi.

The doctor forgets his medicine bag (when he is sick).

Another similar one:

Obuna la nyama, ifaka nd'ekondo.

You fight with a beast (and forget) the knife at your hip.

Mothers' responsibility:

Böna ntaönga, nsoni ea nyango.

(If) the child doesn't do well, it's the shame of the mother.

Industry and laziness:

Ebimb'akaka l'ekalemaka, oleki mbimbi wete ebimb'akaka.

(Between the) industrious and the lazy man, the one who exceeds in having plenty is the industrious man.

When we were young in Africa, we made the blunder of telling mothers how nice and heavy their babies were. Finally a Christian native gave us this proverb:

Nyango afosime bön'ojito.

A mother does not like (the saying) the child is heavy.

This means that a mother never admits that her child is a burden. If she did that, it would be a curse upon the child that would probably result in its death. A child not wanted cannot live.

One day I was working with a group of men and asked one of them for the ax. He said:

Otakundaka eembe ntea wiji bol'etsa.

The one who did not bury the corpse does not know where the head lies.

This sounded impudent and I felt an impulse to say something sharp. However, knowing it was a proverb, I suspended work long enough to get its meaning. It comes from a practice they used to have of giving a man of rank a temporary burial until full arrangements were made for the funeral, which meant hewing out a coffin from a solid log, like a dugout canoe. It was a terrible thing, according to their belief, for one's corpse to be mutilated, especially about the head. Therefore the disinterment, in preparation for the permanent burial, was always in charge of the one who had superintended the temporary burial, for he knew where the head was. That day, when I asked for the ax, the man told me in the most emphatic way he knew, that he had not had anything to do with the ax and knew nothing about it. He had not "buried the corpse."

There is perhaps no other sphere where the Congolese shines quite so brightly as in the role of a story-teller. With his rich, flexible language, his dramatic ability, his powers of impersonation, he makes the stories live before the audience gathered around the campfire in the jungle village. Both animate and inanimate objects seem to move before you as you listen, entranced by the unconscious art of this primitive entertainer.

Among their folk-tales, the animal stories hold a very large place. The following is a translation of a story written by Eonjela, a Christian young man at Bolenge. It was published in the *Ekim'ea Nsango,* a magazine published by the mission in the Lokundo language.

What the Elephant Is Looking For in the Forest

The tortoise borrowed twenty brass rods from the elephant. (Brass rods were formerly used for money in the Congo.) The tortoise did not want to pay the debt and delayed until there was a big palaver over it. The elephant asked repeatedly for his money, but the tortoise did not pay. Then on a certain day the tortoise said, "Look here! You go home and tomorrow morning come and get your money."

The next morning the tortoise called his son and said, "Take your big knife and dig a hole for me and I will be buried, but you leave my back protruding above the ground and you shall whet your tools on my back, pretending it is a whetstone. When the elephant comes, say to him that your father arose before day and went to get the rods for him."

When they had done this, behold, the elephant came and said to the son, "Where is your father?" And the son told the elephant just what his father had instructed him to say. The elephant was very angry and searched to see whether the tortoise was hiding anywhere. Then the son said again to the elephant, "See, I am sharpening the tools. Father and I are going to the garden. He said he would not be gone long. Wait, he will be back soon." The elephant was very angry and searched again to see whether the tortoise was hiding anywhere. Then the son said again to the elephant, "See, I am sharpening the tools. Father and I are going to the garden. He said he would not be gone long. Wait, he will be back soon." And the elephant was exceedingly angry and said, "I am tired of the promises of the tortoise. I am going to throw his whetstone away into the forest." And he seized the whetstone and threw it away.

But what the elephant threw away was the tortoise himself. The tortoise then went around another way, picked up some rods, and came forth and greeted the elephant saying, "You have come, you have come! Here, I am ready to pay you my debt." Then the tortoise looked over where the whetstone had been and of course he did not see it. He called his son and asked him where it was. The son said, "The elephant threw it out into the forest." Then the tortoise demanded that the elephant return his whetstone. The elephant went out and searched diligently for it, but even until now he had never found it and he believes he owes the tortoise a big debt for the loss of a whetstone. And have you not seen the elephant searching around everywhere in the forest?

Why the Leopard Is Afraid of Bees

The leopard and the gazelle were at one time great friends. Then a drouth came, followed by a great famine. The leopard and the gazelle were so hungry that they decided to eat their mothers. This kept them alive until the rains came and there was again plenty of food.

The gazelle got to thinking of his mother and finally decided to make a journey to the City of God to bring her back. He bought him a metalliphone (a small musical instrument the Africans carry and play as they journey along the jungle path).

108

(Here the story-teller imitates the tones of the instrument by saying: *"Ngwi, ngwi, ngwi."* Then all the listeners sing the chorus: "I'm going to the City of God to bring back my mother." As often as he repeats the *"Ngwi, ngwi, ngwi,"* they will sing over the chorus. The story-teller must be clever enough to give each character —animal, bird, or insect—introduced into the story, a part in harmony with the known habits or characteristics of that animal or bird or insect. People in the audience have the privilege of introducing characters. The story-teller must be a keen student of nature to work each character into the story. The characters used here are those that were in the story when I first heard it.)

The gazelle started off on his journey, playing and singing *"Ngwi, ngwi, ngwi,* I'm going to the City of God to bring back my mother." As he journeyed on, he met a spider. (An African story-teller might pause after "met" and give anyone a chance to introduce any character he might choose.) The spider said, "Good morning, gazelle. Where are you going?" "I'm going to the City of God to bring back my mother." "Let me go with you," said the spider. "All right, come on, I'm glad to have your company."

They started on together, singing, *"Ngwi, ngwi, ngwi,* I'm going to the City of God to bring back my mother." After a while they met a butterfly. The butterfly said, "Good morning, gazelle. Where are you going?" The gazelle answered, "I'm going to the City of God to bring back my mother." "Let me go with you." "All right, butterfly, I shall be glad to have you." The party started on, singing, *"Ngwi, ngwi, ngwi,* I'm going to the City of God to bring back my mother."

109

(The story-teller would give in full details the meeting with each new character: dragon-fly, stag-beetles, white ants, and a mouse. The whole party then continues the journey, singing the refrain.)

Eventually they came to a river, deep and swift and wide. There was no bridge or canoe. While the gazelle was worrying how he would ever get across, the spider climbed up on a bush and spun out a web. It floated across on the morning breeze and caught on a bush on the other side of the river. Then over and back, over and back, worked the spider until he had woven a bridge, over which the whole party passed in safety.

The journey was resumed as they marched to the same refrain, "*Ngwi, ngwi, ngwi,* I'm going to the City of God to bring back my mother." One day they came to a large village from which many paths led off in every direction. When they inquired for the road that led to the City of God, they were told that it was forbidden to tell. They would have to find it themselves. The butterfly that flies this way and that soon found the right road and informed the gazelle. They lost very little time and were soon on their way again.

After many days they came to the gates of the City of God. There a messenger informed the gazelle that he would have to find the house where he was to stay. The dragon-fly, with his sharp eye, flew away and soon found the place and led the gazelle and his party to it. The house was so dirty that the gazelle would not enter. The stag-beetles said, "Don't worry." They entered and rolled all the filth up into balls and rolled them outside and the house was clean. Then a messenger arrived to inform the gazelle that he would have to cut down the trees back of the house before he could get his mother.

He appealed to his party and the white ants went out and worked all night. When the morning breeze arose, the whole forest fell flat.

Then the gazelle and his party were shown a large room in which were three baskets. He was told that his mother was in one of the baskets, and he would have to choose the right one, for he could not open it till he arrived back home. The gazelle was worried lest he might take the wrong basket. He looked at one basket, then another, then the third, but could not tell. In the meantime the mouse slipped around behind the baskets and gnawed a hole in each until he found the gazelle's mother. He whispered in the gazelle's ear and they returned home carrying the right basket.

When the gazelle arrived at home he could not get the lid off the basket. So he called the wise men—the witch-doctor and the magicians; but none of them could open the basket.

A hunchbacked boy of the village came along and said, "Hello, gazelle, what seems to be the matter?" The gazelle replied, "I have brought my mother home from the City of God and I can't get the basket open." The boy asked, "Do you mind if I try?" "I certainly would be glad for your help," said the gazelle. Thereupon the hunchback went through with some kind of magic and off came the lid, and the gazelle had his mother.

When the leopard heard about it, he said: "If the gazelle can do that, I can. I'll go to the City of God and get my mother." He bought a metalliphone and started off playing and singing, *"Ngwi, ngwi, ngwi,* I'm going to the City of God to bring back my mother." Soon he met a spider. The spider said, "Good morning, leopard. Where are you going?" "I'm going to the City of

God to bring back my mother." "Let me go with you," said the spider. "You?" said the leopard. "Why, you little, insignificant nothingness, get out of my way! I don't want to be bothered with you." (The story-teller relates how the leopard thus rebuffed and refused the friendship of each one of the characters that had made the journey with the gazelle.)

When the leopard arrived at the river, he had no friendly spider to build a bridge for him. Finally, in desperation he jumped in to swim across. He nearly drowned, but made it across. When he reached the village with the many paths he spent many days in finding the one that led to the City of God. When he reached the city, having no dragon-fly to help him, he spent a long time searching for the house where he was to stay. Then he had to stay in the dirt, for he had no stag-beetles to clean the house for him. When informed that he had to cut down the forest behind the house, he went out and gnawed all night, but did not get one tree down.

Eventually he was led over to the big room with three baskets and told he would have to choose the one that held his mother. "My mother was a big woman," he said. "This largest basket must be the right one." He picked it up and carried it back home. He could not open the basket, so he called the wise men, the witch-doctor, and the magicians, and they all failed. The hunch-backed boy offered to help, but the leopard said, "Go on away. I don't want to be bothered with you." After many unsuccessful attempts to get the lid off the leopard finally had to send for the hunchback. When he came, he said to the leopard, "Are you sure you want the basket opened?" "Of course. My mother is in there.

Open it up." The hunchback said, "If you will take on you and your posterity the consequences of whatever comes out, I will open it." "Go ahead," said the leopard. The hunchback went through with his magic. Off came the lid and out came a swarm of bees. And that is the reason that leopards are always afraid of bees.

PART III

CONGO'S OLD AND NEW FAITHS

CHAPTER I

OLD BELIEFS AND PRACTICES

WHEN WE WERE on our way up the Congo River the first time, our steamer stayed one night at Bolobo, a station of the British Baptist Missionary Society, and we were entertained in the home of Mr. and Mrs. James Clark. During the course of the evening, Mrs. Clark led us into an adjoining room and showed us a baby's bed. It was a basket about the usual size used for such purposes and made beautiful and comfortable as only Christian womanhood knows how to make them. There was a beautiful white mosquito net hanging over it. As Mrs. Clark pulled the net aside, we tiptoed up to see what she had in the basket, and there we beheld one of the cutest little chocolate-colored babies I have ever seen. She told us the story of the little fellow, whom they had named "Philipo (Philip)."

The mission had sent a native evangelist out into the back country and one day he came into a village just as a funeral ceremony and burial was taking place. He went to where the crowd had assembled and found that the mother of this baby had died. They had already placed her in the grave and were in the act of putting the baby in the grave, alive, to bury it with its mother. He asked for the baby, but they refused. He kept on pleading, and finally told them that he would take it to his white *mama* at the mission station, for he knew that she would take care of it. At last they gave him the baby and he took it to Mrs. Clark.

Why did they want to bury the baby with its mother? Do they not like children? Would no one in the village give it a home? The Africans love children above everything else in the world, and perhaps there was not a family in the village that would not gladly have taken the infant and reared it as their own, but for one thing. That was the fear of the return of the spirit of the dead mother. If they kept her baby from her, she would be lonely and might come back to take vengeance on those who had deprived her of her child. It was the kindest thing for the mother, and the safest thing for themselves, to send the baby with her.

For the Bantu, the world is full of spirits, good and evil—spirits of the river, spirits of the forest, spirits of the swamps, spirits of the storm clouds, good and bad spirits. But the spirits that they fear most, and that enter most potently into their everyday life, are the spirits of their own dead. These are their divinities. They are, of course, tribal and local. The Bantu worries but little about the gods of other tribes. He has troubles enough with his own.

So in the case of Philipo, when the evangelist proposed to take the baby to the mission station, that was a happy solution. For if the spirit visited anybody in anger it would be the missionaries; but since they were of a different tribe and lived in a different locality they would have nothing to fear. In our logical way of thinking we would immediately trace the responsibility back to those who gave the child away, but things are never pressed to a logical conclusion in the Bantu's superstitious beliefs. There is no logic in primitive religion.

The dominant impulse of the Bantu religion is fear. The deceased live in the spirit world in the same relationship to each other as they did here in the flesh. Chiefs here become chiefs there, ordinary clansmen here are ordinary clansmen there, and the state of freedom or slavery, riches or poverty, is carried over into the spirit world. The spirits have the same passions—love, hate, jealousy—that they had when living. If a man is feared here, his spirit is to be more intensely feared when he is dead. If a man is easily displeased here, greater caution must be taken when he is gone.

Every precaution must be taken to keep the dead in a good humor. If the deceased is a chief or man of high rank, no pains or expense are spared in making a great and spectacular funeral. Presents are brought to be put in the grave, or in some cases in houses built over the graves. Formerly, slaves and wives were buried, oftentimes alive, with a chief. They represented his wealth and position and he would have them in the spirit world to serve him. Thus he would be more contented and less likely to return to trouble the living. Dancing and singing of flattering songs to the deceased go on for weeks. The more the man has been feared, the greater the funeral

119

and the more flattering the expressions of love and simulations of sorrow.

In some places the nearest relative will get up early each morning for a period of weeks after the funeral and talk to the spirit of the departed by means of the village drum. He will sing his praise in the most flattering terms, professing love for him and deepest sorrow at his going.

Our most remote station up the Tshuapa River is Mondombe. At one time while the whole staff of the station was away for a few weeks at a conference, the chief of the nearby native village of Mbelo died. The funeral was held during our absence. When we returned we found the village greatly troubled. It was an unusually dry season and the gardens were not growing. Hunters were unable to kill any game. After due deliberation as to the probable cause, villagers decided that the departed chief was angry because the funeral had not been adequate for a man of his standing. They therefore staged a second funeral. They built a new house for the dead chief, larger than any other in the village. They decorated it with palm fronds and invited all the related clans to join in the celebration. Crowds came bringing presents which they heaped in the new house, and they all sang and danced for weeks.

The spirits of evil men are much more apt to return to molest the living than the spirits of good men. The spirits may work independent of any body, but they are sometimes incarnate in such animals as crocodiles or leopards. Animals that attack human beings are thought to be possessed by some evil spirit. Many months after the death of the big chief of Mondombe, a boy was taken by a crocodile on the mission beach. The son of the dead chief, who became the ruling chief, sent word to me to be sure to warn our mission employees and school boys about going in the river. "That crocodile that stays in these waters around here," he said, "has the spirit of my father and will kill anyone who goes in this part of the river."

The Bantu of the High Tshuapa bury their dead in a sitting position with the knees drawn up close to the chest. Before the interment they tie two sticks to the side of the head. These they leave protruding above ground from eighteen inches to two feet. If after the burial things are not as prosperous as they should be in the village, they suspect the spirit of the recently deceased person. If they are unsuccessful in hunting, they will sprinkle the grave with the blood of a chicken. If they hunt again without success, the witch-doctor will shake the sticks fastened to the head as a warning to the spirit that he had better quit "tying up" the animals in the forest. If after repeated trial they are unable to kill any game, they open up the grave and the witch-doctor takes the head, rubs some kind of concoction on the forehead of the skull, then slips out into the jungle and hides it. No worse thing than this could be done to punish a spirit. If the hunting still continues to be unsuccessful, they will then seek the cause elsewhere.

Witchcraft is natural in such a realm of ignorance and superstition as Congoland. A witch is one who uses extraordinary or supernatural powers in an antisocial way, and the word is used without reference to sex. The witch is believed to employ occult powers in getting extraordinary wisdom, accumulating riches, stealing, causing others to be sick, but above everything else, in killing people. Witches have power to quit their bodies and assume any form they may choose. They wander about at night, executing their diabolical work of "eating the souls" of men, women, and children. The victims may not be conscious of what has happened, but as their real life is gone they will soon die. People may be witches without knowing it themselves, leading a perfectly normal life in the daytime, while at night their spirits quit their bodies and fare forth on their devilish work. This archfiend and enemy of human society is hated above everything else by the natives.

There is no safety for anyone in a witchbound society. No ties of relationship make one safe from the accusation of the practice of witchcraft. Husbands accuse wives and wives accuse husbands. Children may accuse parents, and parents their own children. One day you may unconsciously stare at someone. If that person should become sick or die soon afterward, someone will be sure to remember that you stared at the victim, and accuse you of "eating his soul" or giving him "the evil eye."

A witchbound society is stagnant. If one is a genius in any way, or accumulates wealth more rapidly than others, he is in imminent danger of being accused of witchcraft and is put out of the way. So the best minds of Africa have often been sacrificed because of this terrible practice.

In such a society, if any thing new or unusual is introduced, and a tragedy happens to follow, the new or unusual is sure to be blamed. Two young women from the mission were making an itinerary among the villages of the High Tshuapa country. One was riding a bicycle. The other was on a "push-push," a chair over one wheel like a bicycle wheel, which is propelled and kept balanced by two men holding shafts that extend fore and aft. They stopped in a village and while they were talking to a group of villagers noticed that others were examining very intently the tracks left in the soft path by the tread of the tires. They thought nothing of it at the time, but not long after their visit someone in the village died. When the villagers cast about for a cause, they could think of nothing else to blame but the bicycle tracks. They worked themselves up into quite a state of excitement, went to the chief and said that because the tracks of the machines from the mission had killed one of their people, they were either going to kill or run out of the village the mission teacher who was stationed there. The chief, however, had been cured of a very serious disease by the mission doctor, so he finally dispersed the mob, declaring that as long as he was chief, the teacher would remain.

No mercy is shown to a witch. It is true that those who are powerful enough in wealth and influence to guarantee their personal safety may sometimes claim to be witches in order to terrorize the people for their own selfish ends. Ordinarily, however, it is very dangerous to admit or to be accused of witchcraft, for it may lead to death by the most cruel and torturous means.

It is in connection with the accusation of witchcraft that the trial by ordeal is most frequently employed. Two of the most frequent forms of the ordeal are the boiling oil and poison tests. In the former the accused must pick some object out of the bottom of a pot of boiling oil with his bare hand. If he is burned he is pronounced guilty, if not burned he is supposed to be innocent. In the case of the poison test the accused person must drink the dose prepared for him. If it kills him, the people are satisfied that they have ridden themselves of another dangerous witch. If the poison purges or produces vertigo, they pronounce him guilty and proceed to put him out of the way. Should he vomit the poison, he is supposed to be innocent, but sometimes he is compelled to take another and yet another dose until he dies and people are satisfied he was guilty. To refuse to take the medicine is to admit guilt. About the only thing that can save one accused of witch-craft is to be in favor with the witch-doctor or to slip him a handsome bribe at night.

On the surface, the trial by ordeal seems to be the most unreasonable procedure imaginable, but it must be re-membered that the village council of former years now meets in the spirit world. All ordinary affairs are tried before the living village council; but in the case of witch-craft there are no competent human witnesses, so it is the most natural thing in the world to appeal the case to the spiritual court. The hot oil or poison is the means by which the spirits render back their decisions. Strange as it may seem, frequently the accused person is the first to ask for a trial by ordeal. He appeals his case to the higher, the spiritual, court.

Fetishes are the means employed by the living to get in touch with the spirits by whom the Congo people be-lieve they are constantly surrounded. By means of fetishes they attempt to get the spirits to act in their behalf, to bring them good luck, good health, and prosperity. They also try to influence the spirits to act against their enemies, causing misfortune, disease, or death. Every house, every garden, every individual, is protected by some fetish, and one must be constantly on guard lest he come into contact with some destructive fetish placed by an enemy to bring him harm.

No number of failures can weaken a native's faith in fetishism. If his fetish signally fails, it is only an indication that some enemy has a more powerful one. He then must pay the witch-doctor to make him one that will outstrip any his enemies may have. This rivalry is a great source of wealth for the witch-doctor, whose greatest skill is shown in the fabrication of alibis to explain the constant failures of his fetishes.

If a man in the Congo has an enemy he wishes to be rid of, he may go to the witch-doctor and have him make a death fetish, to be placed secretly over the enemy's door, or under his bed, or out along the trail where he is likely to pass. If the man enters through the door, sleeps on a bed thus guarded, or passes by the death fetish on the trail, and finds out about it, which he is sure to do, he will die. The death fetish is a serious matter in a country where people still die by the tens of thousands from fear of it. When an African finds that he has violated a death fetish, he is so frightened that it is almost impossible to save his life.

A man who discovered that he had slept over a death fetish was carried up to one of the mission doctors. He was frothing at the mouth and jerking in every muscle of his body. The doctor tried to show him that there was nothing in the fetish to fear. He talked with him, reasoned with him, and did everything he could think of, to no avail. The victim cried out again and again in agony and fear, "O mother, I am dying!" Finally the doctor gave the man a sound thrashing. This "counter-irritant" broke the spell and the doctor was able to save the man's life; but he was left crippled from the mental agony of that night, a case of hysterical paralysis.

The term "witch-doctor" by no means explains the most spectacular figure in Bantu society. He is a witch-doctor, but more than that. The native word *nkanga* means a doctor, a witch-doctor, a priest, a soothsayer, a wizard, a magician, a sorcerer.

The *nkanga* is well skilled in the use of medicinal herbs.

He alone has the occult power which enables him to see spirits and to detect witchcraft. A great *nkanga* holds the power of life and death over every member of the tribe, for by a word he can stir up a fanatical mob against anyone who would dare oppose him. He is a keen psychologist and is very clever in swaying the emotions of the people. Much of his practice is for the good of the community, but many times an *nkanga* stoops to low, selfish, antisocial trickery.

Mrs. Moon and I were once at Bakanga, the little village across the river from the mission station at Bolenge, when they were having a "smelling out" trial. A man had been taken by a crocodile at the village beach and a woman had been killed by a leopard shortly afterwards. The villagers were convinced that someone was practicing witchcraft and was using these animals to carry out their nefarious schemes. They had sent for a famous *nkanga* who lived on the other side of the river, far out in the interior. From the upper deck of the steamer we had a perfect view of the entire village, which consisted of a single row of houses facing the river. The *nkanga* had never been in the village before. Early in the morning he went out into the forest back of the village to put on his hideous makeup. He remained out there for some time, every little while calling out, "I am coming!" At last he came forth and danced up and down the full length of the village a few times like an animated demon. Then he gathered the people together in the center of the village, where he continued to dance, all the while growing more and more excited.

In the center of the circle stood a mat rolled up like a joint of stovepipe. Occasionally the *nkanga* would cautiously approach and look into the mat-roll, then with a scream of frenzy spring away, indicating something of the horror of the thing that was being revealed to him there. When the excitement had reached a high pitch, he suddenly pointed his finger at a young man and said, "You are the one who caused the crocodile to take the man at the beach." The people all exclaimed, "Oh, such wisdom; we might have known that he was the guilty one, for he had been fighting with that man before he was taken." The *nkanga* had never before been there, but he picked out the man in the village most likely to have committed such a deed. And surprising as it may seem, the young man admitted that he was guilty.

The case of the leopard killing was not settled yet, so the trial went on. Directly the *nkanga* indicated a woman as the guilty one, and everyone believed she was, for she had been quarrelling with the leopard victim.

Because this village is so near the mission and the government post, the usual procedure from this point on had to be modified. The villagers did not dare put the victims to death outright or cause them to "take the ordeal," so heavy fines were substituted, to be paid to the relatives of those who had been killed by the animals. The *nkanga* levied the fines somewhat as follows. Speaking to the young man, he said, "You must pay a bag of salt." The man said, "I have no salt." The *nkanga* looked him in the eye and said, "Go into your house and get the salt you have on the smoke-rack." The people marvelled, "How did he know the salt was there? He has never been in that house." The *nkanga* went on levying a number of blankets and pieces of cloth and several thousand brass rods. Each item the man denied having, but he was told by the *nkanga* how many he had and where he kept them. The same procedure was followed in fining the woman.

All this time the people were growing more and more bewildered at the wisdom of the *nkanga*. He had never been there before, but he picked out the two most plausible people in the village. He knew just how much wealth they possessed, and where they kept it. To the missionaries sitting on the deck of the steamer, it was as clear as day. While the *nkanga* had never been there before, the chief of Bolenge village on the other side of the river used to spend weeks at a time at Bakanga. He knew every quarrel and misunderstanding that had recently taken place in the little village, and every bit of wealth the people had and where it was concealed. Before the *nkanga* crossed the river for the trial he went to Bolenge and lived with the chief for two weeks, gathering from him the "supernatural" information with which he astonished the villagers.

The office of witch-doctor is usually kept within a family, the witch-doctor choosing a son or nephew or other near male relative to whom he reveals the science and tricks of the profession. Occasionally, however, a man is clever enough to break into the game. In one tribe on the Congo a man managed to disappear and was gone for some time. When he reappeared, the first time the people saw him he was coming up out of the river. They were astonished and asked where he had been all the time. He told them that he had been down under the river talking to the spirit of the river, and that the spirit of the river had made him a great witch-doctor. The people believed him and he was clever enough in his practice to get away with it.

The question naturally arises in one's mind: "Are these people so simple that they never see through the deception of the witch-doctor?" It is probable that all through the ages certain men have seen the trickery of the *nkanga,* but no man ever lived to accuse a second one of fraud, for the witch-doctors have always been able to turn the wrath of the people against anyone who questioned their practices.

CHAPTER II

A NEW FAITH TAKES ROOT

THE QUESTION that should be of supreme interest to every white man going into Africa is: "What should be the attitude of missions, governments, and commerce and industry toward the native religion?" The first impulse one has, when he sees some of the terrible religious practices there, is to tear out these false beliefs, root and branch; to smash all the false and give them the true. However, in a society that is as fundamentally religious as that of the Bantu, one must consider carefully before he begins a work of destruction, lest he destroy old forms of control before he has made effective the new. A poor religion is better than none. This can be illustrated by a hypothetical case, though one which is typical of what has gone on for years in Africa.

A trader goes into Central Africa, taking with him a

wealth of trade goods—cloth, beads, brass jewelry, hoes, axes. He sets up a small store and sells his goods daily to the natives as he buys from them in turn rubber, ivory, gum copal, palm oil, and other products of the country which he exports to Europe. He takes as a servant a boy who is fresh from the back country and has had no previous contact with white men. The boy comes with his native charms or fetishes. The trader asks him what they mean and laughs at him when he explains. Day after day the trader ridicules the boy's superstitious beliefs and assures him that there is nothing to that world of evil spirits that he fears. As proof he points to the fact that many natives may be found around the trading center who have given up such beliefs.

It is not easy to ridicule the religion out of an African, but the constant daily attack makes its impression. One night the boy sits down and thinks like this: "I never stole from my neighbor's house, for it had a fetish over the door and I feared the spirit would get me. I never stole from his garden, for another fetish was there. The white man says there is nothing in the fetish and there are no spirits to get me. Before I came here I never knew there was such wealth in the world as the white man has in his store. I would like to have some of it. He says there are no spirits to get me, so all I have to do is to outwit him." Some morning the trader finds his keys have been slipped out, the store-room opened, and his servant and all the wealth he could carry have gone to the jungle. The trader curses black men in general, and his ex-servant in particular, saying that they are all thieves—it is born in them and they can never be changed.

Who made that boy a thief? Who deliberately broke the only control he ever had? Admittedly it was a poor control, but it was adequate for the society in which the boy lived and was much better than none.

This illustration may be over-simplified, but it is essentially true of what has been going on in Central Africa for years. The large concentrations of detribalized natives in Africa are often hot-beds of crime, thievery, anarchism, and licentiousness. Every vestige of tribal control has been destroyed and nothing has been given to take its place. That, in brief, is the destructive method which has been so often employed, sometimes unwittingly, even by those who have loved the African best.

Over against this destructive method is the constructive one—an attitude of sympathetic appreciation of Bantu culture, a desire to save anything that is worth while and a reluctance to destroy any forms of control until they have been replaced by something better. Some government officials and traders have been champions of this method and have cooperated heartily with Christian missions in building up a constructive program for native education. Since the problem is fundamentally a religious one, the missions are in a unique position to demonstrate such a method of approach.

The dominant impulse of the native religion is fear, and the people can never advance while they are bound by it. However, to break their fear is to break their control, unless it is replaced by that higher control which is love. They already have a vague belief in a supreme being, one who created everything, but who now, they believe, manifests little interest in his creation. The Congolese look upon him as a benevolent being. They seldom if ever pray or sacrifice to him. They say: "Why should we? He isn't going to hurt us. We are not afraid of him." The logical thing to do, then, is to bring back this absentee creator in the form of a loving Father. This is all the more easy because their ideas of him are very vague, and he has not been corrupted, like gods in other lands, by human intimacy.

The natives' world of evil spirits need not be attacked. The people need only to be assured that even though the spirits were as thick as the leaves in the jungle, they need have no fear. Their loving Father is the supreme spirit, and if they trust in him, he will care for them even as they love their children and would let no harm come to them that they could prevent. When a native is thoroughly indoctrinated with that one truth, he has been changed from a cringing creature of fear to a man of trust who can look the world in the face.

He is then in a position to be taught. For instance, he has always believed that high water was caused by the angry spirit of the river. The only way he knew to make the river go down was to bind a man and drown him in the stream as an offering to the angry spirit. Should you try to explain to him the cause of the high water, he would be afraid to listen, lest the spirit should be angry at him and upset his canoe the next time he ventured on the river. But after you have anchored him to God's love, you may talk to him about the heavy tropical rains that fall at certain seasons along the tributaries of the Congo, causing them to rise and in turn fill the main river to overflowing. He listens, believes, and understands, because you first allayed his fear.

Some sections of Congo have been almost depopulated by sleeping sickness. Like other diseases, it is thought to be caused by evil spirits, and the people fear to talk about it lest they should be the next victims. But if they believe in a God of love, you may take them to the dispensary

and by means of the microscope show them the trypano-
soma, the germs which cause the sleeping sickness. Then
you can explain how the germs are carried by the *tsetse*
fly, teach them how to protect their bodies from the bite
of the fly, and assure them they will never have sleeping
sickness if that fly never bites them. They listen now and
gradually begin to act. Thus through faith in the God
who loves them, the realm of evil spirits is pushed farther
and farther away. Fear and fetishism give way to the
higher control of love.

Something of the power of this new faith in the lives
of the Congo people is seen in the following incident. In
the early days of our mission at Monieka, while the native
preacher was away visiting other villages, the witch-doctor
made a death fetish and put it over the preacher's door.
Friends went far out on the jungle path to warn the
preacher against going near his house where the death
fetish had been hung. He said, "Follow me and see what
I am going to do with that fetish." As he passed through
the long streets of the village he called to the people to
follow. By the time he reached home there was a great
crowd about him. He stood before his house and taught
the people for a while, then reached up for the fetish.
As he did so the people held their breath, expecting to
see him drop in a fit of agony. Instead, he tore the fetish
apart, put that which was supposed to be the deadly
inner part into his mouth, and chewed it up, laughing at
the terror of the people. That one fearless act did much
to break the power of the witch-doctor in Monieka.

From the very beginning the Congo Mission was
strongly evangelistic. When we had but one station we
had a regular routine for our Sunday program. One of
the missionaries would meet the Sunday school teachers

at an early hour and go over the lesson with them. Sunday school attembled at ten. Classes were held out under the orange, mango, and palm trees. Worship and communion followed at eleven. Then the Sunday school teachers separated and, with groups of Christians to help, went to as many villages as they could reach in the afternoon. Some groups went in canoes by river, others over the forest paths. Thus the Sunday school was reproduced in a great many nearby villages. It was reported in those days that Bolenge had the largest Sunday school in the world. In the sense of a single gathering it was never true, but counting the aggregate number reached each Sunday by this one group of teachers, it may have put in a strong bid for first place. This same method has been used at other stations and at out-station centers.

The Congo people are eloquent speakers and marvelous story-tellers. As soon as they become Christians they are encouraged to tell others. They find great joy in telling the Bible stories, and when educated some of them develop into really great preachers.

One morning at Bolenge when I went out to call the roll of workmen and appoint them to their tasks for the day, a youth in his teens stepped up and asked to be enrolled. He gave his name as Bofeko. He proved to be a very faithful workman. He went regularly to all church meetings and whenever work permitted he was in school. After some months, one morning when I called the roll Bofeko did not answer. No one seemed to know what had become of him. I supposed that, like many another, he had boarded some passing steamer and had gone down river to one of the larger towns.

Months passed with no word from Bofeko. At that time Monieka, some two hundred miles up the Busira

River, was becoming an increasingly important out-station. The native preacher there was Nkumba. One day Nkumba was passing through an outlying village where the Catholics had entered. When the Catholic catechist saw the preacher, he called to his followers: "There goes that Protestant. Let's beat him up." They began to attack him with their clubs. The other villagers saw the unfairness of it and rushed out with their weapons to rescue him. In the midst of the fight, a third party led by a young man came into the village. This group took in the situation and drove the Catholics off. Then their leader said, "Hello, Nkumba! I don't suppose you know me, but I remember you. I spent several months at Bolenge and saw you there. I am Bofeko."

Yes, there was the workman who had disappeared from Bolenge. He had gone back up river and out into the back country to his home village. There he had begun to preach to his own people. He started a school to teach them to read and write. The villagers were so impressed that they put up a building for a church and school. The group of men with him that day were some who believed what he had been preaching and were coming to the mission to be further taught and baptized. This is typical of what has often happened in Congo. Some Christian has disappeared, to be found later far out in some forest village letting his light shine to the best of his ability.

The Ubangi River, the great northern branch of the Congo, flows into the Congo about forty miles below where the Equator crosses it. On the north bank of the Congo a few miles above the mouth of the Ubangi, is the village of Bonkombo. The story of Bitumba begins in this village. The inhabitants of Bonkombo belonged to the Bobangi tribe. One of the chief's wives, however, came from the Nkumdo tribe, from a village up beyond Bolenge. She became the mother of Bitumba, who was heir to the chieftainship of Bonkombo.

When Bitumba was a lad in his early teens, his father sent him with some of the village men to the government post some forty miles up river, to deliver the fish tax. Because they did not take the full amount of the levy, Bitumba was held as a prisoner. After a time the white administrator in charge of the post took a fancy to his young prisoner and made him his personal servant. While working for this official, Bitumba learned to speak the French language.

When the administrator's term of service was finished, Bitumba went with him down river and later shipped on a trading steamer as a wood-cutter. One night Bitumba fell and cut his foot severely on his axe, and was not able to get his supply of wood. The next morning he was beaten so severely by the captain for his failure that he was stricken with a long illness. At port, friends took him in and cared for him until he recovered.

When he was well enough to travel he took passage on another steamer to return to Bonkombo, for he had heard that his father was dead. The journey was a hard one. The boat ran aground and when the passengers were helping to push it into deeper water, Bitumba's traveling companion was seized by a crocodile and was never seen again. Smallpox broke out and eleven of the twenty-two people on board died. Bitumba was one of the fortunate ones to recover.

When he reached the home village, he found that his father was alive and was planning for his son's future. He had bought a number of wives for him, whom Bitumba refused, much to the astonishment and displeasure of his father.

About that time the little church at Bolenge sent out its first full-time paid evangelist. He was Ekakula, the maternal uncle of Bitumba, and he was sent to Bonkombo. Bitumba went to the school which was started there and listened regularly to his uncle's preaching. When he told his father that he had decided to go to the mission school at Bolenge, the father was so angry that he threw a spear, intending to kill his son. Bitumba jumped aside. The spear struck the house, and Bitumba suffered only a badly cut foot as it fell. The father died shortly after this incident.

It was not long until Bitumba made full surrender to Christ. In the face of the ridicule of his many friends, he freed the wives and slaves his father had left him and gave up the place as chief of the village.

After receiving what education he could at Bolenge, Bitumba returned to his home village as a teacher, but he encountered much persecution there and it seemed unwise for him to remain. The mission then gave him a small salary and some salt with which to buy food and sent him to the village of Bakanga, opposite Bolenge, to preach and to teach school.

When he paddled up to the beach at Bakanga in his small canoe, the people met him and asked him what he wanted. He told his mission, but they said they did not want him there. Every time he came near, they pushed his canoe away from the shore. He persisted in trying to land, and in the pushing the canoe was swamped and his salt and some other belongings were lost. He managed to save the canoe, and finally the people allowed him to enter the village. However, they refused him a house. Night after night he stayed in the open, in constant danger of crocodiles, leopards, and elephants. He carried on his work until the people would let him have no more food. Then he crossed the river to get a new supply. On the return journey his canoe was sunk by a hippopotamus and he was stranded in a tree on a submerged island for two days before he was rescued by a passing canoe.

For two years Bitumba preached and taught in Bakanga, in spite of his trials and the opposition of the people. At the end of that time he had a little church of fifteen members.

The years went on and Bitumba continued as teacher and evangelist. He was especially interested in educational work and schools flourished where he was in charge. In Ikengo the school work grew until the village had the largest number who could read and write of any village in the district. At one time there were thirty-three full-time preachers and teachers who had begun their education in his school at Ikengo.

He preached by deed as well as by word. Once when on an itineration he came to a village where a man had just died and the people had refused to bury him. Bitumba took his own clothing as a burial robe and gave the body a respectable burial. He had to continue his journey wearing only a loin-cloth, but this act won the people to him, even though they could not understand why he should manifest such kindness. The report of what he had done preceded him to the other villages and he was greeted by large crowds eager to hear of the teaching that so changed men's hearts that they loved even strangers.

In 1914, Bitumba began work among his own tribal

people along the Ubangi River. He was made district evangelist and before long had many outposts up the Ubangi and the Ngiri that flows into it from the east. It took about fifteen days to paddle from Bolenge to the end of the district, but the evangelist made the trip every three months, visiting all the villages. When there were hundreds of Christians he knew every one by name.

With the care of all the churches in this great territory, and the hundreds of new Christians to guide, Bitumba still found time to explore new sections. When he first went to Lobolo the people refused for a time to let him and his companions stay. After considerable argument, the chief gave his consent for them to sleep in the village. Before many days Bitumba bought a site, erected a house for a teacher, cleared some land, planted garden, and began the erection of a church. Then he left the work in the charge of another.

In March, 1917, he was returning to his work from Bolenge, having in his canoe the salt and salary he had just received for the quarter, besides some personal goods which he had never moved to his new location. The canoe was upset by hippopotami and all was lost, leaving him nothing but the clothes he was wearing. Bitumba wrote me of this loss: "At first I was very sorrowful, but soon the thought came to me that it is not the perishable things of the body that count, but the things of the spirit. Then I felt great joy and thankfulness for God's wonderful deliverance from the many dangers in which I have been cast. I may see hardships, but I shall not be sorrowful, but shall rejoice in the name of my Savior."

Thus through dangers and hardships this pioneer preacher opened up a great district to the gospel. We now have several thousand Christians there and in 1945 a new mission station was opened at Bosobele on the Ngiri River to serve this area.

From Mondombe we sent out two young married couples to begin work in a village. At first they were well received. Then some people began to stir up sentiment against them and one day the chief advised them to leave, as the warriors were getting out of control. They refused to go. The next day a war party surrounded their house. As one of the women ran across an open space between their living quarters, a poisoned arrow barely missed her, catching in her skirt. Frightened, she screamed, "I have been killed!" Just then a heavy tropical storm burst on the scene and the warriors withdrew. Realizing then how serious the situation was, the four young people lost no time in getting back to the mission.

Evangelists were sent to the village again as soon as conditions made it possible. Later from that village a boy came to the mission station to work and go to school. His name was Ntange. He learned rapidly and became an exceptionally fine penman. He went on to the Congo Christian Institute at Bolenge. I was in America when he was graduated. He wrote me: "Dear teacher, I have never forgotten what you used to tell us in school at Mondombe. You said that the missionaries could come out and build mission schools and prepare us as preachers and teachers, but you could not preach and teach in all the villages. If that work was ever to be done we would have to do it. I have now finished my college work and am going back to give my life to preaching and teaching among my own people."

With his education and his fine penmanship, Ntange could have gone to the government or to trading companies and found employment which would have paid

him far more than he will ever receive as a preacher or teacher. He is now pastor at Mondombe and has a great influence throughout that whole area. On a recent trip among the villages he baptized more than one hundred sixty people.

Enguta was another evangelist. While preaching out in the forest villages, he contracted an incurable disease. He was carried into the station and placed in the dispensary. The doctor did all he could to relieve his suffering. One day we realized that the end was near. Friends and relatives of the sick man had crowded into the room, and some of us missionaries were present, quietly waiting for the end. Suddenly, with that strength that sometimes comes to people in the last moment of life, Enguta arose to a sitting posture. He exhorted his people for some time in a wonderful way. Then he began to sing, in his own language, that beautiful old hymn:

> O happy day that fixed my choice,
> On Thee, my Savior and my God,
> Well may this glowing heart rejoice,
> And tell its rapture all abroad.

He sang every stanza through, lay down, and in a moment was gone. As I stood looking into that dying man's face, I could see all the terrible dark background of heathenism from which he had come. I could feel something of what it meant to him in joy and life and hope when he sang "O happy day that fixed my choice." That hymn has never been the same to me since that day.

On one overland trip in the equatorial forest region W. R. Holder and I came one evening to a large village, Mbandaka. It was our custom to hold services each evening in the village where we stopped for the night. Since both Mr. Holder and I felt a little indisposed, we decided to call on one of the Christian carriers to preach. I spoke to a young man by the name of Basele, one of the several members of the S.S. *Oregon* who were making the trip with us. I had never heard him preach, but I knew he would, for he had been a Christian several years. You can call on almost any Congolese who has been a Christian for a few years and he will preach any time, any place. Some are better preachers than others, but they are all willing to try.

We were camped in the large oval usually found in the center of the village. It is the chief's compound and the center of village life. Around the edge of the oval were the low thatched-roof houses. Banana trees rose above the roofs and back of the gardens was the dark forest wall that enclosed everything. From the ends of the chief's compound the village streets led off in opposite directions.

After supper we carried our chairs out and sat in the middle of the oval. The Christian workmen gathered about and began to sing gospel songs. Soon a crowd had gathered in the bright African moonlight. After a prayer Basele stepped out to begin his sermon. Around the mission station the men usually dress in white drill or duck suits for service, but out on these trips it is hard for them to take their good clothes along. The usual evening dress of a carrier after a hot day on the trail is a small trade blanket around the waist that falls down to the ankles. Thus Basele was dressed that evening—just the blanket, no shoes and no shirt. He began to speak.

He gave as his text: "Take your house out from under the limbs of the tree." I knew it must be one of their proverbs and listened closely to learn what it meant. In this forest region where the lightning often splits trees asunder and the windstorms blow them down or break off large branches, it is very dangerous to build your house within falling distance of a large tree. When they build their villages, it is a careless man who leaves a large tree standing near. In hunting and fishing camps huts are put down in the heavy forest, and many tragedies result from falling trees.

"It's a beautiful tree," said Basele, "that you have left standing. It has large and spreading branches, and casts a cooling shade over your house and yard. You sit there in the shade and say, 'Isn't it wonderful that I have this shade to enjoy! Look at all those foolish people down the street. They have cut down their trees and are sweltering in the sunshine while I have this beautiful shade over me.' Yes, friend," continued the preacher, "today you seem to be enjoying yourself; but remember this, the thing you are enjoying today, tomorrow may be your destruction. Take your house out from under the limbs of that tree."

Then Basele went around the tree and catalogued the limbs as the great sins those people are most heir to. He would describe the sin and the great thrill they seemed to be getting out of it. As he went from limb to limb, from sin to sin, he preached the greatest evangelistic sermon I have ever heard in any language by any preacher. And how he drove home again and again that same truth! "Yes, friend, today you seem to be enjoying yourself; but remember this, the thing you are enjoying today, tomorrow may be your destruction. Take your house out from under the limbs of that tree."

One day at Bolenge I looked out on the wide expanse of the Congo River and saw a small canoe coming across, with one person in it. The canoe came ashore and an old woman stepped out and walked up the path. "White

Man," she said, "I have come to be baptized." "That's fine," I replied. "What is your name and where do you come from?" "I am Ekota Nganga. I live in Mpombo." Mpombo is a small village about fifteen miles across and a little down the river from Bolenge. Evangelists often stopped there to hold services on their way to larger towns beyond.

I sat down with Ekota and asked a few questions to see if she understood what she was doing. In answer to the first question she said, "White Man, I don't know that, but I do know that Jesus died for me." To each question she gave the same answer. She seemed so completely in earnest that I finally said, "You dear old soul, if you have grasped that one fundamental truth, that Jesus died to save you, that is enough for you." Upon her simple, child-like faith I took her down to the river and buried her in Christian baptism.

After her baptism I said to her, "Ekota, you are too old to live all alone at Mpombo. You had better stay at the mission where you can go to church regularly and where the Christian people will look after you." She looked at me in astonishment. "White Man, I couldn't do that. I must go back and teach my own people. I am the only Christian there."

She returned to Mpombo. As the time for the regular quarterly gatherings at Bolenge approached, we would always see Ekota Nganga coming across the river in her little canoe. The canoe would be loaded with bananas, sweet potatoes, yams, cassava, and other garden produce, Ekota's offering to the church. One day the canoe had two old women in it. Ekota came up beaming with joy. "I am not going to be alone now, for this woman has come to be baptized." After that they always came together until the other woman died and left Ekota alone again. I asked her again to stay at the station, but she refused and went home to her people.

After we returned to America, Ekota fell sick. The mission brought her to the station, where she was cared for during her remaining days. As the end drew near, she said: "I am not afraid to die. I know in whom I have believed. But now that I am going, who will teach my people?"

CHAPTER III

A MISSION STATION
IS OPENED

FEW THRILLS in missionary experience can equal that of being chosen to launch out into unoccupied territory and begin a new station. That joy came to Miss Goldie Wells and Mrs. Moon and me when the time had come to begin work at Mondombe. We made the ten days' run up the Tshuapa River on the *Oregon* and tied up at a sandy beach in front of the chosen site. We spent that night on board.

Early the next morning our baggage, tools, and provisions were unloaded and we stepped ashore, together with a few natives from our older stations who had come along to help us get started. The steamer untied, turned around, and headed down stream. We waved good-bye, knowing it would be many months, perhaps an entire year, before it came again. There we stood, five hundred miles from the post office, and half that far from the nearest doctor should we need any medical attention. And how terribly we did need it before it finally came!

As the steamer went out of sight we turned around and faced the jungle and our task. We knew what kind of people lived there. We knew that just a short time before, in a village a few miles up river, they had killed and eaten two victims and were wearing the dried hands as charms around their necks. We had our baggage picked up and carried about three-quarters of a mile up a narrow trail to a crudely built, unfinished mud house. That was to be our residence until we could put up a better dwelling down by the river. The house had openings for windows, but no sash or shutters of any kind. Each morning, the first few days we were there, we found fresh leopard tracks on the verandah under the windows. In order to let the fresh air in and keep the leopards out, I nailed slats across the window openings.

This was not my first visit to Mondombe. Some years before, the mission had sent four of us out to make an extended survey of the land and tribes along the great Tshuapa River system, which has well over a thousand miles of navigable waterways. We spent several months studying the peoples and looking for strategic centers for future mission stations. Mondombe was one of the centers chosen and was the first to be permanently opened as a station.

While on the survey trip we had preached each evening in the village where we camped. For the pure joy that comes to one from telling that wonderful story of God's love, there is nothing that compares to the thrill of telling it to people who have never heard it. I shall never forget the evening we spent in Lofimo. We preached to a large crowd and when the sermon was finished a young man, who was squatted down in front, arose and said: "That is a wonderful story. We never heard anything like that. Can't you stay with us always and tell that story till we know and understand it?" I replied: "No, we can't stay. We are in a hurry this time." He pleaded, "Can't you stay ten days, or even five days, and tell us that story over and over? It is so wonderful we can't understand it by hearing it just once." I explained that we were sorry, but that we must go on the next day.

On the morrow when we were ready to take the jungle trail we found that the chief had appointed this young man to be our guide. He stepped out ahead of us and for five hours led the tortuous way along the forest path till we arrived at Bokoko, our next stop. I shall always remember the pleading in his voice as he bade us farewell and turned back to his own village. He said, "Well, White Men, if you can't stay now, won't you come again?" We left him our promise to come back some day or to see that someone else did.

Shortly after the survey trip, Mrs. Moon and I came home for our furlough. We finished our year's leave and sailed from New York, to return to the Congo, the day before the armistice was signed at the close of the first World War. When we arrived in Congo we found the mission had turned over to us the superintendence of the new work at Mondombe. On board the S.S. *Oregon* we sailed up the Tshuapa River again.

When we came in sight of Lofimo we saw that a large crowd had gathered on the high bank to greet us. One young man was dancing around very excitedly. The only one dressed in clothing, he stood out in bold contrast to the others who wore only small loin-cloths or monkey skins. I asked the pilot who the young fellow was. He replied, "That is Matayo." A Congolese takes a new name when converted, usually one from the Bible. This man had taken the name "Matthew," which they call "Matayo." I said to the pilot, "But I don't know any Matayo up here." "Don't you remember," he reminded me, "the young man who squatted down in front the first time we visited this village, and at the close of the sermon begged you to stay here to tell them that story over and over? He was also your guide the next day." I recalled him very distinctly then. I had been telling the story while home on furlough. There he was, the first convert in the High Tshuapa country we had surveyed.

And now we were back at Mondombe to begin a new mission station. On the way up river we had stopped at Lofimo and Matayo had asked to come with us. Of course we consented. Matayo later became a preacher.

One of the first things that happened after our arrival was a visit from the chief and some of the elders, old men of the village. We sat around on small trees about six to eight inches in diameter that had been felled to make the clearing for the house. After we visited for a while, I thought they might be interested in my carpenter tools. I opened the chest and took out a handsaw and began to cut a block off of the end of one of the small trees. When those old men saw the saw cutting into the side of the log, their antics were something to behold. When the Congolese get excited, with their left arm doubled up they strike the hollow formed at the elbow with the palm of their right hand, till it pops like a gun. They repeat over and over their exclamation, *"Mo! Mo!"* and the word *"Kilo."* *"Kilo"* refers to something new or strange, such as they have never seen before. When that first block dropped off one of the old men seized it and said, "That's my chair." I knew I was in for it then. I had to make a chair for every old man there before they would leave.

The people were somewhat afraid of us at first, but when the initial fear wore off they began to come asking for work—boys, young men, and a few older men. Before long there were one hundred thirty men and boys on our work roll. And if anyone thinks it doesn't take some superintendence to keep that number of men and boys working to advantage, when they are using tools they had never dreamed of until they were placed in their hands, he is welcome to try it.

The first big job we undertook was to hew out a path through the jungle from our house down to the river. We made the path thirty feet wide and planted a young palm tree every thirty feet along each side. Long ago those palms grew up and touched their fronds across the path. This is our main station path. We sometimes call it "Mondombe Boulevard."

Our next task was to get out material for a small two-story bungalow which we planned to put up down by the river. We had no sawmill, so all our lumber had to be sawn by hand. We used whip-saws or pit-saws, big six- or seven-foot rip-saws. The log is put over a pit or on a scaffold high enough so a man can stand under the log. One man stands on top of the log and works with the upper handle. He gets all the back-bending. Another man stands under the log and holds the lower handle. He gets all the sawdust. There is no fun at either end of a pit-saw. I know, for I had to work sometimes on top and sometimes underneath the log, while teaching the Congo workmen how to operate it. These men could steer a canoe up and down the crooked rivers. They had done that for generations. But to make a saw follow a straight line on the side of a log was a different proposition. Sometimes, when I had to leave them to see about other work, they would wander so far away from the line that the log was ruined entirely and we would have to throw it away. Fortunately there were plenty of logs in that heavy forest on which to experiment.

Eventually we got in some timbers about eight inches square and long enough for our needs for the framework of the house. Since the timbers were not very straight or uniform in size as they came from our crude sawmill, I made a straight-edge, got out carpenter tools, and put some of the young men to work straightening them up a bit.

We had planned to build the first story of our little bungalow of brick. Our next big job was brick-making. We had no press, so I made some molds, each mold the size for one brick. I taught some of the workmen how to puddle the clay and mold the brick. They were often careless about lifting the mold off and made a good many crooked bricks. I had to keep at them all the time to make them straight. They have a word for "straight," but their ideas are only relative. It seemed that everything we wanted done we wanted "straight." We insisted on making the big path straight, and Mrs. Moon had been trying by their help to plant some straight rows in her garden. After a while you could hear the natives saying, "Straight, straight, straight! What's the matter with the white man? Couldn't he walk along a path if it were crooked, and wouldn't things grow just as well in the garden if the rows weren't straight? And now he wants these little mud blocks made straight. What's he going to do with them, anyway?" I told them I was going to build a house out of them, but they couldn't visualize a house made of mud blocks.

Finally enough bricks were made and dried for our first burning. We stacked them up in kiln form. I chose some of the huskiest of the young fellows for my firemen and we started the fires. When we had them going properly, I said to them: "Now, you keep the fires just like that. Don't let them go down a bit or you may spoil the brick." I went away to see about other work. When I returned I found the men sitting calmly around, the fires gone down. It was not because they were lazy, but because they were afraid. They had never seen so much fire concentrated in one place. They kept warning me: "White Man, that's too much fire. You're going to burn up something. You'd better let it go down a little." Whenever I would leave, their morale would go down and so would the fires. I was exasperated, thinking I was never going to get those brick properly burned.

One night they were all sound asleep when they should have been firing. A leopard walked through the kiln shed just behind where they were sitting and left his footprints on some freshly molded brick. When they awakened and saw those leopard tracks, the way they began to throw wood under the brick was a satisfaction to me. They kept it up until the brick were burned. They probably thought that was my leopard, that I had indulged in a bit of witchcraft and sent it to get them if they didn't work.

When the bricks were cool enough we carried them down near the river to the site chosen for the house. I set the corner stakes for the foundation, stretched the strings for the trenches, and stood over the boys and called

"Straight, straight," while they did the digging. The final leveling-up I had to do myself. Then I had one of the workmen watch me very closely as I started the brick work at one corner. When he seemed to be getting the idea I gave him the trowel. That was brick mason number one. Eventually I had a man started at each corner. When I came back to the first man, he had several bricks in wrong. I had him take them out and try again. That day and the next I spent going from one to the other, teaching them the beginnings of brick-laying. Occasionally I stepped over to see how the carpenters were getting along straightening up the big timbers.

During this time of building we kept to a regular daily program. We would get up at half-past five and have early morning school from six to seven o'clock for the one hundred thirty men and boys on our work roll. We took time out for breakfast, then worked until noon. As is the custom in the tropics, the noon-day meal was followed by a *siesta*. At two o'clock the drum beat, calling the men back to work, and the boys on the work roll and the children from the village to an afternoon school conducted by Miss Wells and Mrs. Moon.

After the evening meal a few natives came to the house to teach us the language. Part of the people here spoke Lonkundo, the language we had used at Bolenge; but most of them spoke a different language, the Ladia. While we were studying Ladia we began translating the book of Mark into this tongue.

One of the rare joys I had in my missionary experience was when I had mastered enough of this language to try to preach in it. We had about half of the book of Mark translated at that time. On a Sunday I gathered the Ladia-speaking people together and read to them the first message they had ever heard from the Word of God in their own language. Then I preached to them for the first time without an interpreter. I shall never forget the thrill of that service. It has been thus that missionaries, in their own weak way, have helped to extend the miracle of Pentecost to peoples of a thousand different languages.

Night after night we were so engrossed in our language study that we remained up until twelve and one o'clock. We were forgetting ourselves in the enthusiasm of the work of building this new station. But one cannot work overtime and get away with it for long in the tropics. Soon the strings began to snap. Mrs. Moon came down with a tropical fever. She was in bed a week and her temperature dropped to normal. She was up one day when Miss Wells and I came down with the same kind of fever. We were still living in the unfinished mud house. There were cracks in the dirt floor you could put your foot in and there were thousands of hiding-places for insects in the rough walls. We killed snakes, scorpions, centipedes, and poisonous spiders. No one could guess how many roaches and crickets lived there. The week I was in bed there must have been a whole family of crickets in every hiding-place in that house, and every cricket kept up a constant "chirp-chirp, chirp-chirp" night and day. I was so anxious to get out of that miserable place that as soon as my temperature dropped to normal I got up and went to the river to see how they were progressing with our new house.

They had been laying brick in my absence. Every time they laid a brick they crowded the string over a little. Each succeeding brick pushed the string a little further out of line. When they got about to the middle of the house, by sighting along by the corner stakes they could see that it did not line up. So after each course they moved the corner stakes! They had the walls up about three and one-half feet and had run out of plumb at the corners about six inches. I was heart-broken.

I stood there that morning under the hot tropical sun, weak and trembling from the fever I had had, while they tore down that wall. I re-set the corner stakes and showed them how to lay brick without crowding the string out of line. Then I went to where the men were working on the timbers. They had taken the hand-saw and cut the timbers in two! Of course the timbers were ruined for the purpose for which we were preparing them. It meant weeks again in the forest to get out more timbers.

Everywhere I went that morning I met with that kind of disappointment. At noon I dragged myself up the long path to "Cricketville" again. My head felt as big as a wash-tub and was beating like a bass drum. I crawled back into bed with a high temperature and stayed there another week.

I never was much of a hand to have the blues, but I had a spell that day. However, before long I got myself in hand and began to talk to the "old man," as the natives called me. I said, "Now look here, Old Man, you can't keep up this pace and get away with it. You will have to slow down a bit or your work will soon be finished in Africa. Remember this, these boys aren't starting where you did, in your father's carpenter shop, but—relatively speaking—back about two or three thousand years ago. They can learn. Just be a little more patient with them at the beginning."

When my temperature dropped to normal again, I put a smile on my face and went whistling down the path, ready to meet anything. Things had gone a lot better this time, and we began to make real progress. The basement story of brick was finished, the second story raised and a thatch roof put on, and it began to look like a real house.

The story of the house soon spread out among the jungle villages, and people from days away came in groups to see the wonderful building. They would stand out in the path and gaze up at this two-story house; then one of the bravest of them would venture up and say, "White Man, are there any houses in Europe as big as this house?" I assured them it was a very modest affair, but they could not believe it. Occasionally one of them would say, "White Man, are you not the smartest man that there is?" I would answer, "No, of course not. There are many smarter men than I." They were not convinced. "We never saw anybody do the things you are doing around here, and we think you must be the smartest man there is."

Our next project was the industrial building. It took about twenty thousand brick. Then followed the church and the first unit of the hospital, the dispensary and surgery. We also completed the brick work for a residence before time for our furlough. Soon the men could take a plumb and level and lay up as true a corner as any mason. They could lay the arches over windows and doorways. The best one of the masons became the foreman of the brick-laying squad and the best one of the carpenters became foreman of that group.

All this time the educational and evangelistic work was growing and demanding more and more of our time. We had sent out a few preachers and teachers, but an ever increasing number of villages were asking that we send them Christian leaders. One day the chief of Yongole, a village several days' march to the northward, met me on the station path and asked for a preacher for his village. I did not have anyone ready to send out at that time, so I fenced for time. "Chief, we couldn't send anyone to preach in your village unless he had a church in which to preach." He said, "All right," and walked away. A few weeks later he was back. "The church is ready," he said. "Where is the preacher?"

We still had no preacher to send, so I tried for more time. "That's fine, chief, but if we send a preacher and teacher he will have to have a house in which to live." Again with an "all right" he went away. Before many weeks he was back. "The church and the house are ready. Now I want my preacher." He would have had a preacher that time if I had had to go myself!

There was only one man at the station who was in any measure ready to go, and that was the best apprentice carpenter I had. He was saving me more work than any man then employed at the mission. I hated to lose him. But in a way I had promised the chief, so we outfitted this carpenter with Bible, school materials, and salt with which to buy food, and sent him to Yongole. I told myself I would not make any rash promises to the next chief who came wanting a preacher!

By this time Dr. and Mrs. Ernest Pearson had joined our staff. That night we all talked and prayed over the situation and decided to make a special effort to prepare men and boys to meet the growing demand for teachers and preachers. The next morning I went to the early morning school we had for our employees. Most of the one hundred thirty men and boys had been baptized and many of them could read and write. In my talk I challenged them with the growing demand for preachers and teachers. I told them that preaching and teaching in the village was their job and if it was ever done some of them would have to do it. Then I asked all who wanted to give their lives to that kind of work and begin at once preparation for it, to come forward. We had thirty life recruits that morning. That day we started what we called "The Mondombe Evangelistic Training School." We began to prepare preachers and teachers as fast as we could. They were by no means college graduates when we sent them out, but we did give them a fairly thorough Bible training.

When we sent them out to the villages, they went for a term of five and a half months, then came in for a two weeks' institute in which we tried to further their education. We would send a boy and an older man together. When the boys came in at the end of the term we kept them in the next six months for school and sent other boys out in their places. Thus the boys got six months in school and about six months on the field each year. By that means we kept raising the standard of preparation for our evangelistic force. Some of these evangelists have gone on and have been graduated from the Congo Christian Institute at Bolenge.

The marvelous growth of the work at Mondombe has been in a very large measure due to the consecrated work of these native preachers and teachers. There are now in Mondombe area some 18,000 Christians.

One of the early villages to which we sent a preacher was Yalokosa, three days south of the Tshuapa River. The young fellow sent there had no previous experience. As was usually the case when a man went to begin work in a new village, the chief gave him a warm welcome, a house to live in, and ordered the people to see that he had plenty of food. But it nearly always happens that the preacher, even with his meager education, is soon the important man in the village and people begin going to him for advice. When that happens the chief becomes jealous and turns against the preacher, often becoming just as bitter as he was warm in his first welcome. In this village the chief turned the evangelist out of his house and forbade the people to sell him any food. Being young and inexperienced, the boy could not stand up to the chief and he gave up the post.

By the beginning of the next six months' period we had received a few recruits for our ministerial staff from the older stations down river. They were men of some experience in village preaching. I asked one of them, John Etui, to go to Yalokosa, but he refused. I pressed the matter, telling him that it was an important center and I wanted to hold it for our work. "The chief ran the other preacher out. You are older and have had experience. Why will you not go?" He replied, "You surely know that I belong to the riverine tribe. We never travel overland. I would die with lonesomeness if I got three days' march away from the river." I pleaded with him and finally he agreed to go for one term.

When John arrived at Yalokosa with his wife and two small children, the chief gave him a hearty welcome and a place to live. But before many weeks John was the big man in the village. The chief turned against him, put him out of the house he had given him, and ordered the people not to sell him food. By that time John had friends who helped him build a house of his own and they saw that he and his family had plenty to eat. When it was about time for the next gathering at the mission station, the chief sent out word that if any of them went with the preacher to the mission to be baptized he would put them in chains at hard work. In spite of all his threats, five of the finest couples in the village came to the station for baptism.

When the institute was over and I was going over the roll of villages to see that there was a preacher for each outpost, I came to Yalokosa. Looking around at John, I asked, "How about it, John? Are you going back?" "Going back?" he replied. "Of course I'm going back!" "Well," I said, "I didn't know. You said you would only go there once." He spoke with determination: "That chief is trying to run me out, and I am going to show him he can't do it."

John went back for a second term and the next time he returned he had a large number ready for baptism. At the head of the list was the witch-doctor, usually the hardest man in the tribe to win. With the witch-doctor was his favorite wife, their married daughter, and her husband, and they were carrying the witch-doctor's grandchild.

When these people become Christian they usually want a Christian marriage, even though they may have been married after the native custom for years. The night after the baptisms twenty-three couples lined up in front of the church for marriage. At the head of the line stood the witch-doctor and his wife, and next to them their daughter and her husband.

Again John went back to the village. The church prospered and grew until nearly half of the people in the village were Christians. When the chief continued to fight them, they moved off some distance and made a Christian village. The people in the old village continued to become Christians and to leave the chief to take up their abode in the new community.

Two days farther south from the mission station is a group of five villages known as Mbelo. It would take a long day's travel afoot to make the circuit on the path that joins them together. Early we sent one of our young preachers to work in this group of villages. As soon as people were interested, he enrolled them and required them to come every day for Christian instruction.

Among those who came was an old woman. She was wrinkled and scarred with the cicatrices of tribal marks on her face and body. Her own people tried to dissuade her. They said, "You're too old to learn that new way." She declared, "I'm going to try it anyway." "They don't want an old broken-down woman like you are." But she persisted, "They have invited me and I am going." Then they called in a Catholic catechist. He asked her, "Do you know how they baptize over at the mission?" She did not know. "Well," said he, "I'll tell you. They take you down to the river, put you under the water, turn a canoe over your head and leave you there all night. If you are alive in the morning, you are considered baptized and you belong to them." The old woman was not dissuaded. "I don't care if they do. I am going to find out for myself."

When it was time for the next gathering at the mission station this old woman was among those who came from Mbelo. She had made the five days' trip through the jungle on her feeble old limbs. She was a pitiful sight, but as earnest as any of those who came. On a Lord's Day during the institute this woman and one hundred thirty-seven others stood in line for baptism on the sandy beach where we had stepped ashore from the *Oregon* when we first came up to Mondombe to begin the station. She may have been old and broken and scarred, but there was something beautiful in that homely old face when she came out of the waters of baptism. Something glorious, something divine, radiated from her soul that day. After a few happy days at the station, she went back to her forest home.

When it was time for the next institute she said to the preacher, "I am too old to make that trip to the mission again." But she gave him the best chicken from her flock, saying, "You take this to the white teacher as a parting gift from me. I hear he is going on a long journey to his homeland to see his own children he left there years ago." How often we have thought of and prayed for that dear old soul!

From the moment the doctor joined our staff he was kept busy. At first only the employees, students, and others closely connected with the mission came. Gradually the influence of his medical and surgical skill reached out into the villages round about. I well remember the first major operation. There was no trained nurse to help. In such cases the doctor "drafts" whoever may be available to assist him. On that occasion the doctor asked me to give the anaesthetic and Mrs. Moon and Miss Wells to help in other ways. Untrained helpers add to the surgeon's responsibility, for he has to watch everything the assistants do as well as perform the operation.

We placed a dining-table on the ground floor of the house before a large double door that opened out on the yard, so that the people might stand and watch everything that was done. As the patient was going under the anaesthetic, we heard them saying, "He's dying, he's dying!" When the doctor made the first incision and he did not move they said, *"Aobwa nye* (He is altogether dead)." Then they quietly watched the doctor as he removed an elephantoid tumor that must have weighed upwards of twenty-five pounds.

For want of a hospital, the man was placed in a small native hut near the station. He got along well for a day or two. Then in a dream one of his ancestors appeared to him and told him he would certainly die if he ate any more food in Mondombe. No amount of coaxing, reasoning, or persuasion could induce him to take another mouthful of Mondombe food. His people heard about the dream and came to take him home. They took his dream very seriously and were thoroughly convinced that if he ate anything more in Mondombe he would die. We had to let him go. Giving the relatives some bandages and medicines, which they did not know how to use, we sent him back to his home village, with a prayer that the Lord would yet save this first operative case in that Upper Tshuapa country.

We did not hear from him for months. Then one day a big, husky fellow greeted the doctor and said, "Don't you know me? I'm the fellow you operated on." There he was, sound and well. The Lord had certainly helped in that case. Literally tons of elephantoid tumors weighing from ten pounds to over one hundred pounds each have been removed by our Congo doctors.

Every department of the work at Mondombe prospered and contributed to the one great end of establishing God's reign in the hearts and lives of the forest tribes of the High Tshuapa. In hundreds of villages the drums now call the children to school and devout worshipers to the chapel for prayer. The people that sat in darkness have seen a great light.

SUNSET OR DAWN?

OUR TERM WAS FINISHED and it was time for us to return to America. The *Oregon* came up to get us. It docked at a new beach where the land was about level with the upper deck. After our baggage was put on we stepped aboard and stood on the upper deck holding our three-months-old son, David, facing a large group of Christians who had gathered on shore to see us off. They tried to sing "God Be with You Till We Meet Again," but before they were through the first verse they choked up with emotion and could not finish it. We stood on deck with tears dripping from our cheeks.

When one unselfishly serves a needy people and sees the wonderful change in their lives, it does something to one's own life. How we would love to see them again! It is not likely that we ever will in this life; but we know that they are a part of the eternal spiritual fellowship that can never be broken. We can still hear their farewell blessing: "*Lokendaka bolotsi-o. Mpacenana lenkina.* (Have a good journey. We shall see each other again.)"

We did not know at the time that this was to be the end of our service in Africa. We have longed to return, but it has not been possible. But some of our missionary comrades of those days are still on the field, and younger missionaries whom we have helped to interest in service in the Congo are now leading our own spiritual children of the forest tribes. The fellowship remains unbroken.

As I pen these lines I am, in mind, again sitting in the cool of the evening at Bolenge mission station, looking

167

to the westward out upon the broad main channel of the Congo, beyond which are many forest-covered islands.

As the sun nears the horizon a cloud bank is piled high in a constantly changing variety of fantastic shapes. On this shifting scene that great artist, the sun, is lavishly spreading a wealth of color that must tax even the infinite supply at his command. Here and there through crevices in the clouds he reaches with giant brush and tints with glory the scattered clouds in the eastern sky. Then with one last stroke he draws his brush across the Congo and leaves a path of pure gold.

In a moment the sun is gone, the picture fades, the cloud canvass is rolled away, and night has come on. A cricket chirps, the night-hawks come forth, great bats silently wheel about on dusky wings, the hoot-owl calls in sepulchral tones to his mate, and presently the jungle which has lain all day in silence under the intense heat is alive with a thousand voices singing hymns of praise for such a wonderful night.

Late on into the night I sit in silence and look up into the sky, which by now is so perfectly clear that the diamond stars seem to have no settings. It is no longer a starry sky, only stars. The sky is gone. As I look, time and space seem to lose their meaning and nothing is left but the infinite and the eternal.

Sunset! There is something of beauty, peace, and restfulness in a sunset that sometimes makes one wish it could last forever. But sunset is not the whole cycle. Darkness follows sunset and out of the darkness we strain our eyes looking for the break of day. And when it comes, who can describe it? There is something grand and glorious in the burst of dawn. Its stirring music of life soon drowns out the evening hymn of peace.

Sunset or Dawn?

Everywhere in Africa there are signs of daybreak. The people are emerging from darkness into new light and new life. They are becoming conscious of this world in which they live. A large air field now lies near our base mission station in Congo, and mission-trained native engineers service the planes that land there—planes that link the heart of Congoland with Europe, Asia, and America. It is a day which the missionaries knew was coming and for which they have worked feverishly to prepare the people.

In the Congo, mission work has been marvelously successful. Few mission fields at home or abroad have shown such rapid growth. The fifty years of the Disciples of Christ Congo Mission along the Equator has been almost one continuous Pentecost. Nor has the growth been in numbers alone, for the deepening of spiritual life and the training for service have kept pace with the numerical strength.

From the beginning we have placed great emphasis on the education of the Congolese. Since their language had never been written, we had to begin at the very foundation. Both ignorance and fear had to be overcome in teaching even the alphabet. Letters, which to them at first were curious marks that could talk, and inspired only fear, now speak intelligibly to thousands. In the beginning an untaught native feared nothing more than the threat to write his name. Now hundreds of village schools, the higher mission station schools, and the Congo Christian Institute constitute an educational system that is disseminating spiritual and intellectual light and truth. Whole communities are being transformed.

I would not leave the impression that all Congo people who profess Christianity are saints and live perfect lives

169

ever after. Some come to the church for ulterior motives. Some run well for a while, then fall by the wayside. But when all has been said, there are thousands of reborn men and women in the Congo. To the missionaries, who know the dark background from which they came, many are living testimony to the power of the gospel. Reports telling of the baptism of hundreds and thousands of Congolese are continually coming to hand.

But that does not tell the story of the continuing battle with heathen practices and beliefs. Recently a young man came to missionary Ned Roberts and Ntange Timothy, the native pastor, with this story. He was the son of an *"nkanga ea nyama,"* a witch-doctor, whose specialty is appeasing the spirits so that hunters will be sure of meat. According to custom, upon his father's death he would take his father's place. But he had become a Christian and no longer believed in such practices and refused to pretend to do so. He was taken on a hunt to see if he had his father's power. Within a few minutes he had killed a wild pig, proving in the eyes of the heathen that he was the man for the job. He still refused and was dragged before the native chief and judges. When he resisted their persuasion, he was thrown into jail. Still he did not change his mind. He now came to the leaders of the church seeking help, that his people might be persuaded of their errors and be brought to the Christian way of life. He had become practically an outcast because of his stand, but chose to remain with his people to prove that followers of the Christ have "the way of life." The Christian leaders say: "We earnestly believe and pray for his success as a 'hunter of men' rather than a 'hunter of meat,' knowing he has found the life that is more than meat for the body."

Sunset or Dawn?

From the beginning, medical work has played an important part in the development of our mission. Besides the service to missionaries in looking after their health and thereby increasing their years of usefulness, our doctors have served government officials and traders and raised the mission work in their favor. Of course, the primary and greatest service of the doctor is to the native people. He has relieved suffering, raised the standard of health, and often been the means of breaking down prejudices. Many superstitious beliefs and practices have fallen before the teaching and practice of our doctors.

The surgeon's knife has been the key to many a closed door. In new fields natives sometimes ask to be paid to take the first dose of medicine. It takes a great deal of assurance to persuade the first one to undergo surgery, and superstition often jeopardizes the life of the patient.

With a hospital at each major station, staffed with a doctor and nurse, health and hygiene are being taught, clinics are held for mothers and babies, and groups of native nurses and medical assistants are being trained. When trained these assistants carry valuable medical help to thousands in the back country. There are now important leper colonies conducted by our mission near Lotumbe, Mondombe, and Wema.

What a field for the consecrated Christian doctor the Congo is! Every day's work presents a new challenge to his skill, his faith, and his energy.

The Congo was never more in need of effective missionary service than now, and the opportunities were never greater. I speak of need because before the people have been freed from their primitive fears and superstitions they are being called upon to meet European culture, often in its most blighting form. Opportunities

171

are great, for strategic centers have been occupied throughout the area and the natives are still very responsive to the gospel message.

The nine mission stations of the Disciples of Christ, and a large and growing Christian community, constitute a notable beginning. But it is usually easier to start a work than to carry on through the years, easier to win people from paganism than to train them for citizenship in the Kingdom of Heaven. If our Congo mission is to continue its outstanding evangelistic program and at the same time continue to train native leaders to take over an ever increasing load of responsibility in carrying on the church, there must be a great increase in the number of missionaries.

A careful study shows an urgent need to double the present number of missionaries. There are now openings for almost every type of trained workers: doctors, nurses, teachers, builders, agriculturalists, printers, and ministers. Every missionary, whatever his special training, is primarily a proclaimer of the gospel message. Missionaries do not become pastors, but we need men with the very finest biblical and ministerial training to teach native pastors and evangelists.

Sunset or dawn? The work of redeeming Africa is just begun. The darkness is still great. Everywhere the blackest of heathen practices stand in bold contrast to the spots of Christian light. Not so long ago a young missionary couple was married at one of our stations. It was a beautiful church wedding. The ceremony was first read by a native pastor and the vows taken in the Lonkundo language. Then it was repeated by one of the missionaries in English. Afterward the happy party proceeded on the S.S. *Oregon* to the nearest government post to attend to certain legal phases of the marriage.

When they were about ready to continue their journey down past the capital of the district to Bolenge, the government official asked if he might send some prisoners down with them. They consented, and thirteen prisoners were brought forth. The official said, "These are hunters who were unsuccessful in the chase and who seized two children and ate them." The government, with all of its watchfulness and severity, has not been able completely to stamp out some of these darker practices. It will take the light and love of the Lord Jesus in the hearts of the people.

Sunset or dawn? Missions must make it *Dawn*. The sins of Western materialism are gripping Africa everywhere with their blighting curse. At what tremendous cost has Africa fed the insatiable greed of the West! The slave trade cost her one hundred million lives. The Congo rubber raids took uncounted thousands. What will be the next chapter of the story of the white man's exploitations in Congoland?

The colonial government has for years shown a genuine concern for the development of the Congo people, and many traders and agents of large companies are wise and sympathetic in their dealings with them. Even so, with the rapid development of the material resources of the country the Congolese are apt to be overwhelmed until they see no values except in material things. Unless there is an intensive program of moral and spiritual education, they will be left in a worse state and farther from the Kingdom than they were when in their old heathen life with their primitive cults. It rests with the churches of the West to make the notable beginning they have made indeed the dawn of a brighter day in Congo.

The world knows of the rich agricultural and mineral wealth of the Congo, and men can be found any day who are willing to go out to exploit these resources. The missionaries know not only the deep spiritual needs of the Congolese but they also know of their possibilities for intellectual and spiritual development. The redemptive power of the gospel among them has been abundantly demonstrated. Shall we rest content with past achievements or press on to new victories? God's children of the Congo forest are saying, "Come over and help us."

Eight days' march beyond our most remote station, I once climbed to the top of a hill. It was but four hundred feet high, yet it was the highest in that region. A trader had cleared the forest from the top of the hill and had built himself a house. Standing there I looked back over the dense green forest blanket which covers every acre of that vast region. Here and there I could see smoke spires which marked the sites of villages hidden in its dark recesses. I thought of Moffatt's challenge that took Livingstone to Africa, "I have seen the smoke spires of a thousand villages where Christ has never been preached." Today there is still a vast number of villages in the great rain-forest area of Central Congo where Christ is unknown.

God still speaks as he did to Isaiah in the temple, "Who will go for us?" And loyal souls still respond, "Here am I, send me."

The text of this book is set in 12 point Baskerville. Composition, printing, and binding: Von Hoffmann Press, Inc.; drawings and jacket design: Louis LeVier.